THE DAM BUSTERS

Dedication

For my dear father

David Dunbar Falconer

19 April 1934–8 January 2002

THE DAM BUSTERS

BREAKING THE GREAT DAMS OF GERMANY, 16-17 MAY 1943

JONATHAN FALCONER

First published in 2003 by Sutton Publishing
This edition published in September 2010
by Haynes Publishing

A catalogue record for this book is available
from the British Library

ISBN 978 1 84425 867 3

Library of Congress control no. 2010924928

Published by Haynes Publishing,
Sparkford, Yeovil,
Somerset BA22 7JJ, UK
Tel: 01963 442030 Fax: 01963 440001
Int. tel: +44 1963 442030
Int. fax: +44 1963 440001
E-mail: sales@haynes.co.uk
Website: www.haynes.co.uk

Haynes North America Inc.,
861 Lawrence Drive, Newbury Park,
California 91320, USA

Design and layout by James Robertson

Printed and bound in the USA

Contents

Foreword

Richard Todd OBE – 1919–2009

I had the honour and good fortune to be cast as Guy Gibson in the epic film *The Dam Busters*. Preparations and research for the project had lasted two years before filming started in 1954, and during that period I readied myself to play Gibson by discussions with his widow, his father, various acquaintances and former members of 617 Squadron, besides reading all the material I could get hold of, including of course his own book, *Enemy Coast Ahead*, and Paul Brickhill's *The Dam Busters*, on which the film is based.

I wish now that Jonathan Falconer's book had been available to me. It would have added greatly to my knowledge and understanding of the events of the night of 16–17 May 1943, and the preparations for and aftermath of that historic attack on the great dams of western Germany.

A wealth of detail and meticulous research has been encapsulated into Mr Falconer's book in such a very readable style that I have read and re-read the work with enthusiasm and real pleasure.

I am sure that this latest description of the dam busters will be riveting for all those who take a keen interest in Second World War history, in the achievements of RAF Bomber Command and in the British film industry.

OPPOSITE *Richard Todd as Wg Cdr Guy Gibson in the film* The Dam Busters. *(Studio Canal)*

LEFT *Michael Redgrave and Richard Todd on location at Scampton during the making of* The Dam Busters.

Acknowledgements

Four books have been invaluable to me in researching and writing this short account of 617 Squadron's dams raid. Of these, the two most important were Guy Gibson's own account of the build-up to Operation Chastise and the attack itself, in *Enemy Coast Ahead*, first published in 1946, and John Sweetman's *The Dambusters Raid*, first published in 1982.

Enemy Coast Ahead covers the whole of Gibson's RAF operational flying career with 50, 29, 106 and then 617 Squadrons. His account of the dams raid itself is, therefore, a fairly short appreciation, occupying only three chapters out of eighteen, albeit from the unique perspective of the leader of the raid and one who was actually there. However, there is now some speculation as to whether some of Gibson's writing was guided by the hidden hands of ghost writers at the Ministry of Information and Air Ministry. Even if this is the case, *Enemy Coast Ahead* still makes compelling reading because it is the story of one of Britain's top bomber pilots of the Second World War, and positively reeks of the atmosphere of the period.

John Sweetman's *The Dambusters Raid* is a scholarly and highly detailed account of the background to Chastise, the attack and its aftermath. This book is probably as good as it gets about the dams raid, in terms of both depth of research and level of detail incorporated into the narrative. Not only has Sweetman consulted a wealth of primary sources of information during the course of his research, but he has also interviewed many of the survivors of the dams raid – back-room boffins and 617 Squadron ground crew, as well as Barnes Wallis and aircrew survivors themselves.

Paul Brickhill's classic, *The Dam Busters* (1951), and Helmuth Euler's *The Dams Raid through the Lens* (2001) were also of considerable help to me. Brickhill researched *The Dam Busters* soon after the end of the war, when many of the main characters were still alive and the momentous events they had helped to shape were still fresh in their minds. Euler's work is very much the dams raid as seen from the German perspective. First published in German in 1992 as *Wasserkrieg*, it is the story of the raid through the lenses of the photographers who recorded the Chastise story before, during and after the operation, supporting many fascinating German eyewitness accounts.

It is a great privilege to have the foreword for this book written by the distinguished film and stage actor Richard Todd, who played Guy Gibson in Michael Anderson's stirring account of Operation Chastise, *The Dam Busters*.

The photographic archive of the former Road and Transport Research Laboratory is a truly massive and engrossing pictorial resource that only now is beginning to see the light of day. Hopefully, once this material has been assessed and catalogued, it will be available to a wider audience beyond the civil servants and road engineers for whom it was intended. I am very grateful to Richard Ibbitt, chief photographer of TRL Ltd (formerly the Road and Transport Research Laboratory), for allowing me access to some of this incredible collection, and for his interest in this book.

Margaret Jones and Kinnie Desai of the National Physical Laboratory at Teddington are also to be thanked for tracking down a photograph of No. 2 Ship Tank in which Barnes Wallis carried out trials on golf-ball-size models of the bouncing bomb. The photograph is reproduced by kind permission of the Controller of Crown Copyright.

Paul Couper AGAvA is the talented illustrator responsible for the fabulous three-view scale drawings of the Avro Lancaster B Mk III (Type 464 Provisioning). Paul is available for commissions and can be contacted at http://www.paulcouper.co.uk

Thanks are also due to fellow authors and enthusiasts: Dr Alfred Price, the late Bruce Robertson, and Richard Simms, for searching their own photograph collections and for allowing me to reproduce illustrations obtained from these sources; Graham Pitchfork for assistance with gallantry awards information; Ian Thirsk at the RAF Museum for his ready assistance with some points of detail concerning the film *The Dam Busters*; photographer and author Richard Winslade for permission to reproduce the superb photograph of the BBMF Lancaster; and the acclaimed aviation artist Nicolas Trudgian and the Military Gallery, Bath, for kind permission to reproduce Nick's two wonderfully evocative paintings.

I am grateful to Paul Baillie, military researcher, who procured copies for me of the award citations for Guy Gibson and Ken Brown from The National Archives (Public Record Office).

My much missed late friend and former work colleague Bow Watkinson was a great source of advice and guidance when it came to picture selection. Thanks are also due to him and to another former colleague, Martin Latham, for creating the diagrams and maps that appear in this book.

John Herron of Studio Canal was enthusiastic and helpful in tracking down stills photographs from the film *The Dam Busters*, and for providing copies of the original film poster and souvenir book from his company's archives. They are reproduced here by kind permission of Studio Canal.

The Bundesarchiv, Germany, the Imperial War Museum, London, the RAF Museum, Hendon, Atlantic Syndication, PRM Aviation, Jarrod Cotter and the Royal Society (Godfrey Argent) have also been very helpful in providing many of the photographs that illustrate the pages that follow: the photographs from their respective collections are reproduced with their kind permission. In the case of the museums, individual copies can be obtained by contacting the relevant institutions at the addresses below and quoting the full negative reference number.

Bundesarchiv
Potsdamer Strasse 1, 56075 Koblenz,
Germany
www.bundesarchiv.de

Imperial War Museum
Department of Photographs,
Lambeth Road, London SE1 6HZ
www.iwm.org.uk

RAF Museum
Photographic Department,
Hendon, London NW9 2LL
www.rafmuseum.org.uk

Introduction

Thanks to a 1955 film called *The Dam Busters* that thrilled cinema audiences the length and breadth of Britain, a wartime exploit of an elite RAF bomber squadron assumed legendary status almost overnight. It is doubtful whether any other RAF squadron – or indeed any flying unit in any other air force – could have achieved such fame for a single operation, then or now. The squadron in question is, of course, No. 617, and the operation was the attack in May 1943 by nineteen Avro Lancasters on the Möhne, Eder and Sorpe dams in western Germany, using Barnes Wallis's revolutionary bouncing bomb.

In the eyes of the wartime British press, and later of author Paul Brickhill and the Associated British Picture Corporation, 617 Squadron and Operation 'Chastise' (as the attack on the Ruhr dams was code-named) certainly had all the ingredients of a classic war story – a miracle weapon, an eccentric inventor, a secret squadron formed from the very best crews the RAF could muster, and a seemingly impossible task of destroying a clutch of hitherto unassailable targets. Success in the task would almost certainly alter the course of the war; but the end result was a pyrrhic victory. Two of the three main targets were destroyed, a Victoria Cross was awarded to the squadron's gallant leader, and an unsustainable casualty rate saw nearly half of 617's crews killed. The horrendous aircrew losses bore out Bomber Harris's warning that low-level attacks using heavy bombers were recipes for disaster; but

the raids moved the irascible bomber baron to grudgingly acknowledge the justification of Bomber Command's existence that they so clearly upheld.

Born sixteen years after the war's end, I have no direct personal experience of the famous dams raid, but, like many boys of my generation, a passion for the exploits of Guy Gibson and his dam busters was stirred through eagerly reading Paul Brickhill's classic account of 617 Squadron at war. In what I believe was its first airing on television, the BBC screened Michael Anderson's peerless film, *The Dam Busters*, over the Whitsun bank holiday in May 1971. At a little before eight in the evening on Sunday 29 May, my father switched on our black and white television set and the family settled down to watch Richard Todd and Michael Redgrave re-enact this epic story. For two hours the film held me spellbound, and its effect on me thereafter was deep and far-reaching.

Soon afterwards I rushed out to my local model shop in Bath, the Modeller's Den, to buy the Revell 1/72nd-scale plastic model kit of Guy Gibson's Lancaster, G for George. Several years later, when I had a little more pocket money to spare, the giant 1/48th-scale dam buster Lancaster was purchased and, after weeks of careful gluing and painting, it took pride of place in my bedroom. What it was to gaze intently at these inanimate plastic leviathans on my chest of drawers and imagine myself up in the cockpit of G for George, alongside Guy Gibson, with the deafening sound of four Merlins reverberating in my ears, red-hot flak zipping past the cockpit, assisting him with the throttles on the run-in across the Möhne lake.

Over Sunday tea, I recall hearing my grandfather talk about the dams raid and of some of the men involved whom he had known or met during his thirty-four years in the RAF. As an engineering officer during the Second World War he had been closely involved at RAE Farnborough, and then at RAF Benson, with the development of the Spitfire and Mosquito for photo-reconnaissance use. In the course of this work I believe he had met Guy Gibson, albeit very briefly, as well as the PR pilots whom he had known well and who had flown from Benson on the pre- and post-dams raid reconnaissance flights. During the early 1950s my grandfather had also known dam buster Ivan Whittaker when they were both serving with the RAF in the Suez Canal Zone. Whittaker had been Mick Martin's flight engineer on the dams raid.

As a young boy, links with these titans who had moulded aviation history were such stuff as dreams were made of. However tenuous, these associations served to deepen my interest in Operation Chastise, and in RAF history generally. The opportunity to write this book is thus a childhood dream come true.

At this stage, however, I should point out that it is intended neither as the definitive account of the raid, nor seeks to offer new or controversial interpretations. Rather, I hope that the book will be received as an accessible narrative account of the dam buster legend, supported by a strong and well-presented selection of photographs and illustrations. But an added problem to the telling of such a well-known story is the dearth of action photographs depicting the raid itself. Owing to the extreme secrecy surrounding Chastise, only nine official photographs were taken – and these were on the ground at Scampton – before and after the raid, of which only four were passed for publication by the censor. What happened to the remaining five is anyone's guess, although I suspect they were destroyed. Thus, what was probably the RAF's most famous operation of the Second World War became the least photographed. Perhaps this adds to the power of the dam busters legend.

Jonathan Falconer
Bradford-on-Avon
September 2002 and June 2010

BELOW *The 617 Squadron memorial at Woodhall Spa, Lincolnshire, pictured after the 65th anniversary reunion in 2008, when wreaths were laid in the presence of the sole surviving dam buster crew captain, Les Munro.* (Jarrod Cotter)

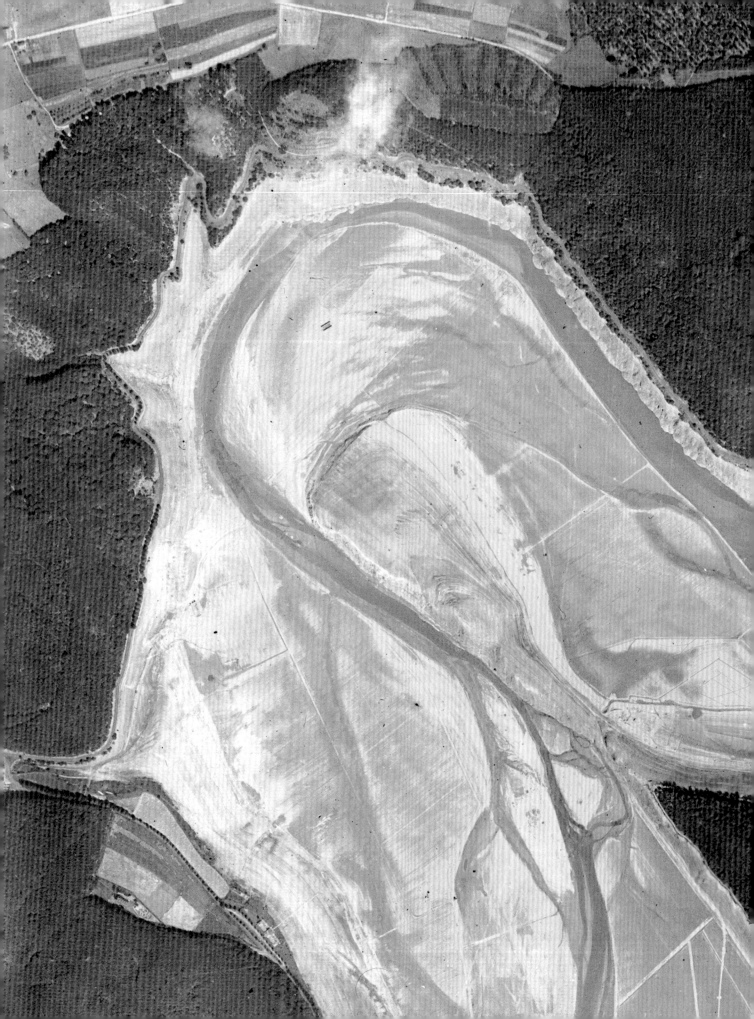

RAF photo-reconnaissance coverage over the Eder Dam two months after the dams raid showed the reservoir (Edersee) was completely drained and dry. On the river bed in front of the breached dam (top right) a light railway had been constructed in preparation for its repair. A new hutted encampment for workmen had also been built to the right of the dam. (IWM C3729)

Prologue

One hour to go, and one hour left before Germany, one hour of peace before flak. I thought to myself: here are 133 boys who have got an hour to live before going through hell. Some of them won't get back. It won't be me – you never think you are not coming back. We won't all get back, but who is it will be unlucky out of these 133 men?

Guy Gibson in *Enemy Coast Ahead*, 1946

Bomber Command have struck deep, and their achievement may well alarm the Reich. Successful air attack on a large dam was considered not long ago impossible. Germany will learn that other things outside the calculations of the Luftwaffe are now possible to the Allied Air Forces.

Leading article in the *Daily Telegraph*, 18 May 1943

OPPOSITE
Devastation at the Möhne dam.
(Bundesarchiv 101I/637/4192/27)

In the early hours of this morning a force of Lancasters attacked with mines the dams at the Möhne and Sorpe reservoirs. . . . The Eder dam was also attacked and reported as breached. . . . The attacks were pressed home from a very low level with great determination and coolness in the face of fierce resistance.

Air Ministry communiqué, 17 May 1943

I was overcome by the immensity of it [the inundation] and when I realised what had happened I just wondered if the powers that be realised just how much damage had been done.

Flg Off Jerry Fray, RAF photo-reconnaissance pilot, 17 May 1943

The British came close to a success which would have been greater than anything they had achieved hitherto with a commitment of thousands of bombers.

Albert Speer, Hitler's Armaments Minister

BRITAIN'S POWER IN THE SKIES

VICKERS "WELLINGTON"
fitted with
"Bristol" PEGASUS ENGINES

THE BRISTOL AEROPLANE CO. LTD., FILTON, BRISTOL.

CHAPTER 1

Striking Back

The RAF's Early Bombing Offensive

Two days after Hitler's forces invaded Poland in September 1939, Britain declared war on Nazi Germany. At home, as the blackout went up and sandbags were piled high, Britons steeled themselves for the war that now lay ahead. While civilians learnt to live with rationing and shortages, the RAF was faced with the problem of how to wage an effective strategic air offensive against Germany with so few and inadequate aircraft: on any given day, only 280 were serviceable and with crews. Air Chief Marshal Sir Edgar Ludlow-Hewitt, then Commander-in-Chief of Bomber

BELOW *A scene of well-ordered activity surrounds this 110 Squadron Bristol Blenheim light bomber at Wattisham in Norfolk as it is refuelled and bombed up for another sortie in the invasion summer of 1940. Blenheims and their crews suffered an alarmingly high casualty rate during the daylight raids against enemy targets in the first years of war. (IWM CH364)*

RIGHT *These Wellington crews of 149 Squadron have just returned to their base at Mildenhall following the RAF's raid on Berlin of 25 August 1940.* (IWM HU44271)

PREVIOUS SPREAD AND RIGHT
Alongside the Wellington, the Handley Page Hampden (previous spread) and Armstrong Whitworth Whitley (right) helped take the war back to the German homeland, until, in turn, they were superseded by the new generation of four-engine heavies.
(IWM CH271/Author's collection)

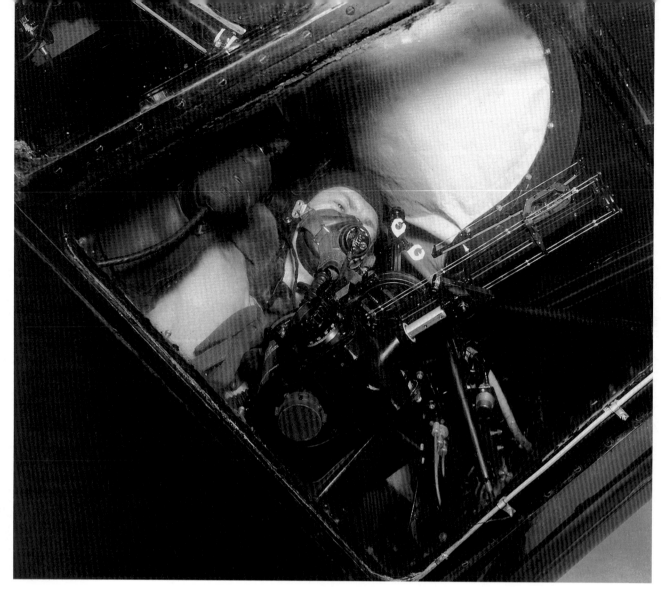

ABOVE *The Butt Report in August 1941 revealed to RAF commanders that few if any of Bomber Command's night bomber aircraft reached their targets, let alone dropped their bombs anywhere near them.* (IWM CH11542)

Command, tried in vain to open the eyes of the Air Staff to the serious shortcomings in aircraft, armament and equipment, and not least aircrew training at even the most basic level. After the first costly daylight bombing raids on enemy targets in September and December 1939, the pre-war theory that the bomber would always get through was quickly proved wrong, and Bomber Command realised that if it wanted to avoid heavy casualties, the only way to pursue an effective bombing campaign was under cover of darkness.

During the winter of 1940–1 it was believed that bombing raids on the small but vital enemy oil refineries in the Ruhr Valley would reduce Germany to impotence. While the attacks proved a dismal failure, the first signs of the future 'area offensive' were in evidence on 16 December 1940, when the centre and suburbs of the city of Mannheim were bombed. By March 1941, however, the U-boat menace in

the Atlantic Ocean had reached crisis point and Bomber Command was diverted for three months from direct attacks on Germany to bomb enemy naval targets elsewhere, in the hope of relieving the wolf packs' stranglehold on the Atlantic convoy supply routes to Britain.

With its aircrew untrained and untried in night bombing, it was not until mid-1941 that Bomber Command was forced to face up to its grave shortcomings. The Butt Report of August 1941, commissioned by Prime Minister Winston Churchill's scientific adviser, Lord Cherwell, revealed that few if any of its bombers had reached what they thought was the target, and fewer still had actually dropped their bombs anywhere near it. Hundreds of brave aircrew had died in the process, and to little effect. But with the formation in 1942 of a specialist target-finding and marking force, 8 (Pathfinder) Group, the first of several measures was taken

to remedy this situation. The Pathfinders' task was to guide squadrons of the main bomber force to the target, which they had marked in advance with coloured flares and target indicators, thereby enabling accurate bombing to take place.

However, the problems encountered by the Command's heavy bomber squadrons of finding and hitting a target by night did not stop the medium bomber squadrons of 2 Group from continuing to mount daring but often costly daylight raids against enemy targets in occupied Europe and in Germany itself: locating a target in daylight and hitting it with bombs from low level did not pose the same problems for navigation and bombing accuracy as a night-bombing operation over a longer distance and at high altitude. From May 1943, control of 2 Group passed from Bomber Command to the 2nd Tactical Air Force, in preparation for the Allied invasion of north-

west Europe, and from there on the Command became an exclusively 'heavy' force.

In the latter half of 1941, Bomber Command suffered increasingly heavy losses. The exceptionally harsh winter that followed was doubtless to blame for some of these casualties, but when on 7 November 1941 thirty-seven aircraft failed to return from a force of 392 despatched, with Berlin as the main target, Churchill ordered that bombing operations be suspended until the following spring. In some respects, this gave the Command a welcome respite, with time to regroup and reassess the direction of the bomber offensive, but it also served to show it up to its critics in the Admiralty and the War Office as being a bottomless pit into which considerable resources had been thrown, to little effect.

However, it was not all doom and gloom for Bomber Command in 1941. The first of the new generation of four-engine bomber aircraft

ABOVE *Locating a target in daylight and from low level did not pose the same problems for the light bomber squadrons of 2 Group, but the danger from flak and fighters was probably greater. Here, smoke rises from the Matford truck factory at Poissy, 10 miles from Paris, following an unescorted daylight attack by Boston medium bombers of 88 and 226 Squadrons on 8 March 1942.* (IWM C2202)

destined to transform its striking power began to come on stream with front-line squadrons, beginning in February with the Short Stirling, swiftly followed in March by the Handley Page Halifax, and by the superlative Avro Lancaster in March 1942. The trio of new heavies gradually replaced the obsolescent twin-engine Wellingtons, Whitleys and Hampdens that had so valiantly borne the brunt of the early offensive.

On 22 February 1942 Bomber Command and the bomber offensive gathered fresh momentum with the appointment of a new and dynamic commander-in-chief, Air Chief Marshal Sir Arthur Harris. Known to his crews as 'Butch', he immediately set about stifling criticism from his detractors by launching the first 1,000-bomber raid in May the same year, against Cologne, which simultaneously proved

to the Germans and some opponents nearer to home in Whitehall that Bomber Command meant business and was far from being a spent force.

During 1942 three scientific research projects began to reach fruition, enabling Bomber Command to radically improve its navigation and bombing accuracy. These were Gee, which first saw use in February 1942, followed later that year in December by Oboe, and in January 1943 by H2S.

Without doubt, 1943 was a watershed for the fortunes of Bomber Command. At this mid-point in the war it possessed a heavy bomber force made up almost exclusively of four-engine aircraft, flown by better-trained crews using the latest in radar technology for navigation and target finding, and guided over

BELOW *Following his appointment as Commander-in-Chief in February 1942, Air Chief Marshal Sir Arthur Harris - architect of the RAF's strategic bomber offensive - set Bomber Command firmly on course to becoming a powerful and effective weapon of war.* (Crown Copyright)

land and sea by Pathfinders, enabling them to drop their bombs fairly and squarely on target, thanks to accurate target marking, improved bombsights and better bombs.

Not all Bomber Command's war efforts were channelled into mass attacks on urban targets. A number of high-profile precision raids on key targets were flown both in daylight and at night by small forces of heavy bomber aircraft. The first deep penetration daylight raid by a small force of Lancasters was mounted against the MAN diesel engine factory at Augsburg on 17 April 1942. Seven of the twelve attacking aircraft were lost and the assault proved a costly failure, reinforcing the fact that in daylight unescorted bomber aircraft were easy prey for enemy fighters. High-risk raids such as this incurred the ire of Bomber Harris, who was vociferous in his condemnation of attacks on so-called panacea targets that were supposed to shorten the war.

Perhaps the most widely known precision bombing raid of the war was that on the Ruhr dams on 16–17 May 1943 by a force of nineteen specially modified Lancasters of 617 Squadron led by Wg Cdr Guy Gibson. With its risky combination of an untried miracle weapon and panacea targets, the plans for Operation Chastise would have been vetoed by Harris and the Air Ministry had it not been for the dogged persistence of Barnes Wallis, the vision of a handful of influential government scientists and the backing of the Chief of the Air Staff. The story of the planning, execution and aftermath of this epic operation is the subject of this book.

BELOW *Bomber Command's trio of four-engine heavy bombers transformed the RAF's striking capability. The Handley Page Halifax entered service in February 1942. This example, a B Mk II of 405 (RCAF) Squadron, is bombing up at Topcliffe in Yorkshire.* (Author's collection)

RIGHT *The first four-engine heavy bomber into service was the Short Stirling in August 1940. These are Stirlings of 1651 Heavy Conversion Unit. (Rover Group 9955)*

OVERLEAF *The third and most successful of Bomber Command's trio of four-engine heavy bombers was the Avro Lancaster. Here, 57 Squadron Lancasters are seen at Scampton in February 1943. (IWM CH8785)*

The **LANCASTER**

CHAPTER 2

The Impossible Dream

Developing the Bouncing Bomb

For some years before the Second World War, the Air Ministry had harboured an interest in the possibility of attacking the large dams in Germany that fed the factories of the Ruhr. By 1937 a list of dams that were considered to be of strategic importance was drawn up, and in the following year the Air Ministry established a Bombing Committee to investigate the possibilities. With the likelihood of another world war looming, a meeting of the Committee on 26 July 1938 concluded that a low-level aerial attack against the German reservoir dams was feasible and should be examined further.

It was no secret to Britain's military planners that the heavy industry, domestic water supplies and river navigation of Germany's industrial heartland in the Ruhr Valley depended to a large degree on water storage in the upper reaches of the River Ruhr. During the Second World War a mighty stream of weapons and munitions flowed from its many factories and foundries to feed Germany's armed forces and the battlefronts on which they were engaged, from Norway to North Africa, and from the Atlantic Wall to the Russian Front.

Germany's reservoirs provided flood protection and during periods of drought guaranteed a minimum water flow in the rivers they fed. They also provided water supplies for industry and generated hydro-electricity. The two most important reservoirs were identified by the Air Ministry as being on tributaries of the River Ruhr – the Möhne and the Sorpe,

with the Möhne reservoir providing more than a quarter of the storage capacity of all the reservoirs along the Ruhr. A third reservoir was on the River Eder, a tributary of the River Fulda, which flows northwards as the River Weser and passes through the industrial city of Kassel. At that time, the Möhne and Sorpe dams provided 75 per cent of the Ruhr's water requirements. If they could be destroyed it would have a catastrophic effect upon German industry, not to mention morale.

When the Möhne dam was opened in 1913 it was one of the largest in Europe. Its elegantly curved 2,133ft-long wall made out of granite masonry blocks employed the latest in construction techniques to hold back 176 million cubic yards of water. Some 43 miles to the south-east of the Möhne lies the Eder dam, which was opened in 1914. Although its wall is 820ft shorter than the Möhne, it is still the largest reservoir in Germany and holds back 264 million cubic yards of water in a lake more than 16 miles long. Nine miles south-west of the Möhne is the Sorpe dam. Opened in 1935, the straight 2,297ft-long Sorpe was for many years Germany's highest earthen dam at 226ft high, and was constructed with an earth embankment around an inner concrete core.

The Möhne and Sorpe dams supplied water for the heavily industrialised Ruhr conurbation, and supply was mainly provided by the extraction of water from the River Ruhr. Owing to the natural flow characteristics of the river and the water loss to adjacent river basins,

the continual demand for water in the Ruhr Valley could only be met by the operation of reservoirs on the tributaries of the River Ruhr. These reservoirs stored water during times of high water flow and discharged extra water during times of low natural flow. The highest flow at these dams was in March, when the reservoirs held back some 176 million cubic yards and 94 million cubic yards of water respectively.

Water was discharged from the Möhne and Sorpe reservoirs during the course of normal operations and was harnessed to produce hydro-electricity in power stations just below the dams. The amount of water discharged depended on water-level requirements in the river below. However, the generation of hydro-electricity at both the Möhne and Sorpe dams was a by-product of the principal purpose of water quantity management. From the main power station, the water flowed into the compensating basin from which it was steadily discharged into the River Möhne via a secondary power station.

In breaching the Möhne dam alone, it was anticipated that a disaster of almost biblical proportions would be unleashed on the low-lying districts of the narrow Ruhr Valley. Large loss of life would be inevitable due to flooding, and industry would be seriously affected by restrictions on its supplies of water. Damage to the transport infrastructure of the region, such as roads, railways, and navigation on the River Ruhr, was also likely.

Between the Möhne dam and the city of Mulheim there were thirteen hydro-electricity generating stations, which would either be completely destroyed by the raging floodwaters, or have their energy production severely disrupted by wild fluctuations in water flow from the reservoir. Heavy industry in the Ruhr Valley – the blast furnaces, iron foundries and coke ovens – would be massively inconvenienced by a shortage of the water that was the lifeblood of their manufacturing processes.

The functions of the Eder dam were unrelated to those of the Möhne and Sorpe, and its primary purpose was flood prevention in the Hessen region. However, to release its 264 million cubic yards of water into the Eder, Fulda and Weser valleys would result in widespread flooding of large tracts of agricultural land and the possible inundation of the low-lying districts of the city of Kassel. The Mittelland Canal also relied upon a water supply from the Eder dam, which was pumped from the River Weser to maintain its levels. Added to this was the almost certain destruction of the four power stations situated in the shadow of the dam, which would have an effect on the operation of the Preussenelektra electricity supply system. On balance, however, it was believed that the consequences of breaching the Eder dam would not be so devastating as those resulting from the destruction of the Möhne and Sorpe dams.

The Air Ministry planners realised that, to be effective, any attack on the great dams of western Germany would need to be mounted during the spring, when the water flow was at its greatest. Experience had shown that narrow structures like dam walls presented very difficult targets to hit when seen from overhead. They were also resistant to destruction from conventional bombing attacks. Thus, the challenge that now faced the planners was how to mount a successful assault when the RAF's existing bomber aircraft, arsenal of bombs, and tactics were clearly not up to the task.

When the Second World War broke out on 3 September 1939, 52-year-old Barnes Wallis was employed as the Assistant Chief Designer of Vickers-Armstrongs' Aviation Section at Weybridge in Surrey. Guy Gibson was later to describe him in his book *Enemy Coast Ahead* as 'neither young nor old, but just a quiet, earnest man who worked very hard. He was one of the real back room boys. . . .' As an aeronautical engineer, his reputation was already second to none through the design of the R100 airship and the Wellesley and

LEFT *Barnes Wallis, inventor of the bouncing bomb, pictured after the war.* (Vickers)

Wellington bombers. On 4 September 1940, when the Battle of Britain was at its height, the Luftwaffe bombed the Vickers factory at Weybridge. Severe casualties and major damage resulted, and Wallis and his design staff were hurriedly evacuated to requisitioned offices in the grand setting of nearby Burhill Golf Club at Hersham, near Walton-on-Thames. At this time, and quite independent of the Air Ministry's deliberations on the subject, it became apparent that Wallis had been working for several months on a number of projects to design air-launched weapons capable of destroying supposedly invulnerable structures, of which the Ruhr dams were high on his list.

Wallis considered the design of bombs currently in use by the RAF and concluded that a 10-ton bomb shaped like a teardrop and dropped into a reservoir within 150ft of a dam wall would have a good chance of fatally damaging the structure. Tests were conducted

OVERLEAF *Aircraft of the RAF's bomber force in the early years of the Second World War were incapable of lifting, let alone accommodating, large bombs. Here, in July 1940, armourers at Scampton prepare to bomb-up this Handley Page Hampden of 49 Squadron with 250lb and 500lb GP bombs. The heaviest weapon it could carry was a pair of slender 2,000lb SAP bombs. Clearly, lifting a 10-ton bomb was out of the question.* (IWM CH272)

Only when the Avro Lancaster entered RAF service in 1942 did Bomber Command come into possession of a potent bomber aircraft that, with modification, was capable of lifting Wallis's 10-ton bomb. This Lancaster served with two front-line squadrons before relegation to a training unit in 1944. (Author's collection)

at the National Physical Laboratory (NPL) in Teddington using a wind tunnel model to determine the likely performance of the new bomb.

Because the RAF's existing bomber force was quite incapable of lifting a 10-ton bomb, Wallis also turned his mind to designing a high-altitude six-engined stratospheric bomber, named 'Victory', to carry the proposed huge weapon. With the encouragement of Vickers, in July 1940 he had attempted to persuade the Air Ministry to approve the development of this ambitious new aircraft.

Disappointingly for Wallis, his enthusiasm was not shared by ministers and officials at Adastral House and 'Victory' never got beyond the drawing board. However, the Air Ministry did acknowledge the need for high-altitude aircraft and large bombs, and requested Vickers to speed up the development of existing aircraft designs to meet these requirements.

Meanwhile, a different set of tests was commenced at the Road Research Laboratory (RRL) in Harmondsworth, under the supervision of its director, Dr William Glanville. With the outbreak of war in 1939, the resources of the Department of Scientific and Industrial Research (DSIR) had been reorganised and the RRL became the principal centre for research on civil defence matters. However, as the war gathered pace, it became increasingly involved in military projects. In October 1940 Glanville formed a small research team headed by engineer A.R. Collins to carry out tests that investigated possibilities for destroying dams. Wallis visited the RRL at this time to discuss plans for the tests with Glanville, Collins and Dr A.H. Davis (Assistant Director of the RRL). He suggested the three main targets should be the Möhne and Eder masonry gravity dams in Germany and the Santa Chiara di Ula multiple-arch dam in Sardinia. (The latter was never attacked even though it was the most vulnerable.)

Also in October, the first in a series of trials was carried out on a roughly built 1/50th-scale model of the Möhne dam to determine whether a big bomb could destroy it. A gravity dam relied on its own weight for stability, and the accuracy of the model test could not be relied upon because it was impossible to scale down the effects of gravity, even though all the dimensions, materials and explosive charges used in the model and the test were accurately scaled down from the full size. The results were not encouraging, and by May 1941 the Air Staff had abandoned Wallis's idea for a big bomb, at least for the time being. However, the RRL continued testing.

Meanwhile, between November 1940 and January 1941, further tests were carried out at the Building Research Station at Garston, near Watford, on a more precisely constructed 1/50th-scale model of the Möhne dam.

A series of ten test explosions was carried out using 2oz charges at a distance of between one and three feet from the dam wall; but the structure held. The tests were later moved

BELOW *A 1/50th scale model of the Möhne dam was painstakingly constructed at the Building Research Station at Garston, near Watford, for experimental purposes. Test charges were exploded close to the inner wall to see what it would take before the structure failed.* (TRL Ltd)

to Harmondsworth, where further trials were undertaken.

Although his initial ideas had failed to find favour, when Wallis approached Dr D.R. Pye, the Director of Scientific Research (DSR) at the Ministry of Aircraft Production (MAP), with his latest theory, he found a receptive mind. Pye sanctioned use of the Road Research Laboratory for a trials programme to assess the effects of explosive charges when placed against or near the wall of a gravity-type dam. An informal committee (the Aerial Attack on Dams Committee) was formed on 10 March to monitor progress and coordinate any developments that came out of the trials.

In the same month Wallis began to examine the destructive characteristics of a bomb, and concluded that the pressure or shock waves occurring in air, earth or water could cause a structure to crack so severely that it would collapse completely. It was widely accepted that gravity dams like the Möhne and Eder, together with earth types like the Sorpe, were particularly difficult structures to breach.

The first two were enormous concrete or masonry structures set on a broad base and with a high wall, triangular in cross-section to give strength. The latter, constructed of two sloping earth and rubble banks encasing a vertical concrete core, was almost invulnerable to direct hits from bombs or the effects of shock waves. However, in all cases, if the dam wall could be fractured by shock waves from an underwater explosion, then there was a strong possibility that the whole structure would fail due to the huge back-pressure of water in the reservoir. The big question was how could an explosive charge be placed

BELOW *The redundant Nant-y-Gro dam near Rhayader in mid-Wales was earmarked as a likely guinea pig for a series of explosives trials against a full-size dam structure. Beforehand, however, a scale model (seen here) was built to test calculations. (TRL Ltd)*

against the inner face of a dam, a charge powerful enough to cause the complete failure of a gravity dam and cause serious leakage in an earth dam?

Further trials involving another 1/50th-scale model of the Möhne dam and the full-size Nant-y-Gro dam in mid-Wales were to prove that the Möhne dam could be breached if 6,500lb of high explosive could be detonated against the inner wall of the dam.

The disused Nant-y-Gro dam was a small structure built out of mass concrete and measured 180ft long. It was straight in plan and had been built across a stream in the beautiful Elan Valley, near Rhayader, to create a one-million-gallon reservoir. Situated as it was in a remote corner of Wales, Nant-y-Gro was ideally placed for the top-secret trials to take place. On 1 May 1942, the first live explosive tests were carried out on the dam, but they did not seriously damage the structure. After further development work, another attempt was made in July of that year when an explosive charge was suspended from the mid-point of the dam at the optimum depth, and detonated remotely. The result was a success: a huge central section of the dam wall, measuring 60ft wide by 24ft deep, was successfully breached.

A key factor in the success of this venture was to ensure that the explosive charge was placed flush against the dam wall. The tests had established that multiple-arch and gravity dams could be successfully breached, but only with a direct hit on the water face of a gravity dam at a specified depth with a single charge of explosive weighing between 7,000 and 9,000lb. A charge that was detonated 50ft from the wall would need some 30,000lb of

BELOW *The real thing: an explosive charge is detonated against the inside wall of the Nant-y-Gro dam in Wales, throwing a huge column of water over the parapet.* (TRL Ltd)

ABOVE *Special measuring equipment was used to gauge the efficacy of the scaled-down explosive charges used against the dam wall.* (TRL Ltd)

OPPOSITE TOP

Nant-y-Gro, 2001. The swathe of pine trees marks the location of the dam wall (in the foreground) and its reservoir. (Author)

high explosive, a requirement clearly beyond the capabilities of the RAF at that time – but a 9,000lb bomb was within the carrying capacity of current aircraft such as the new four-engine Avro Lancaster. The biggest problem lay in achieving the precision of bomb-aiming.

So, how could the smaller quantity of explosive be planted right up against the inner wall of the dam? Wallis set his mind to the problem. In April 1942 he began working on a proposal for a spherical bomb that could be mechanically back-spun by the launching aircraft and released from low level about 400–500yds from the dam face. It would then bounce across the surface of the reservoir until it reached the dam wall and sink to a depth of 30ft, where it would explode. The back-spinning – similar to skimming a flat stone on water in the game 'ducks and drakes' – was important to increase the effective speed and range of the weapon and to ensure that it would rebound when it hit the dam wall and crawl down the inner face before detonating.

In mid-May, Wallis's paper was read by his friend Professor P.M.S. Blackett, Scientific Adviser to the board of the Admiralty and a leading experimental physicist, who was

POINT OF RELEASE – APPROX 400–450YDS UP

DIRECTION OF SP

TORPEDO N

This diagram explains how Barnes Wallis's revolutionary bomb was designed to bounce across the surface of the water, skipping anti-torpedo nets, before striking the inner face of the dam wall and sliding beneath the water to a predetermined depth before exploding and breaching the structure. (Bow Watkinson)

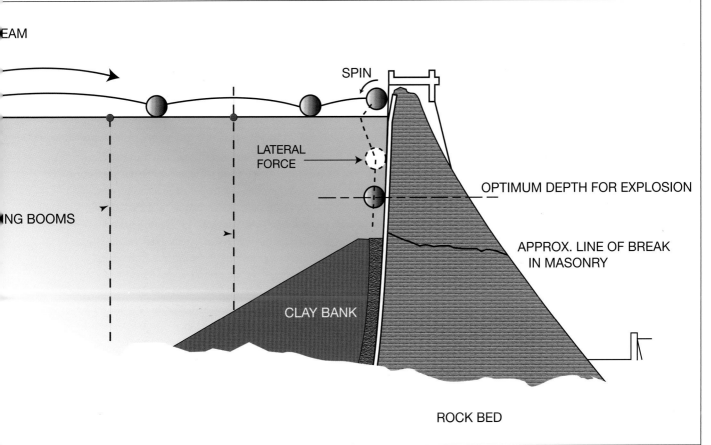

EAM

SPIN

LATERAL
FORCE

OPTIMUM DEPTH FOR EXPLOSION

APPROX. LINE OF BREAK
IN MASONRY

NG BOOMS

CLAY BANK

ROCK BED

ABOVE *The 640ft-long No. 2 Ship Tank at the National Physical Laboratory (NPL), Teddington, which was used by Barnes Wallis to perfect delivery of the spherical weapon that eventually became the bouncing bomb. A selection of spheres the size of cricket balls simulating a full-size weapon were fired from a specially constructed catapult fitted to the gantry over the tank, which can be seen in the background of this photograph. Along with the other water tanks at the NPL, No. 2 Ship Tank was demolished in 1998.* (HMSO/National Physical Laboratory)

impressed enough to pass it on to Sir Henry Tizard, Scientific Adviser to the Chief of the Air Staff. Tizard shared Blackett's enthusiasm, and in early June he authorised use of the Shipping Research Tanks at the NPL in Teddington for further trials. When top brass from the Air Ministry, Admiralty and MAP attended a demonstration of the mine at Teddington on 21 June 1942 they were so impressed by its potential that they immediately sanctioned full-scale live trials.

A number of twin-engine Vickers Wellington bombers were specially modified for aerial trials and six half-size inert prototype spherical mines were built for experimental purposes, fabricated from steel in several different configurations – ribbed, smooth and wooden-clad. Two mines at a time were carried in tandem inside the open bomb bay and back-spun before they were dropped. On 3 December 1942 Captain Joe 'Mutt' Summers, the Vickers chief test pilot, flew Wellington Mk II, BJ895, from the Dorset fighter airfield at Warmwell for the first test drop of the mine off Chesil Beach on the Dorset coast. Lying on the bomb-aimer's couch in the nose of the 'Wimpy' was Barnes Wallis who, when

the time came, pressed the tit and released the mine. Unfortunately, the results were not good because the mines shattered on contact with the water, but a further test flight was conducted on the 15th and the trials continued. On 5 February 1943 the weapon finally proved itself when solid wood mines achieved the desired results and the bouncing bomb, now code-named 'Upkeep', finally became a reality. It was not until late in April that the size and shape of the weapon was finally decided upon.

When the Controller of Research and Development (CRD) at the MAP passed the results to the Air Staff, he cautioned that producing a full-size operational version of the bomb in time to bomb the Ruhr dams in May 1943, when the water levels were at their highest, was out of the question. Instead, he suggested delaying use until the trials of the 'Highball' ship-busting weapon were completed. In any case, there was a danger that secrecy and surprise could be compromised on the parallel development of this spherical weapon if Upkeep went ahead.

It was at this point that Upkeep came close to being abandoned, after Wallis had encountered stiff resistance to his invention

ABOVE *Several specially modified Wellington bombers were used to conduct trials using inert prototype spherical mines. The earliest trials with the dummy weapons were carried out between 4 and 15 December 1942 by Wellington Mk II, BJ895, flown by Vickers' chief test pilot, Mutt Summers, with Barnes Wallis as bomb aimer. Two prototype spherical bombs can here be seen in the converted bomb bay.* (Vickers)

FAR LEFT *Captain Joseph 'Mutt' Summers, chief test pilot at Vickers-Armstrongs, played an important part in the trials of the bouncing bomb.* (Vickers)

LEFT *R.C. (Bob) Handasyde was also closely involved as a flight-test observer in the trials.* (Vickers)

Further trials took place in December 1942 and January 1943 in the Fleet lagoon, the long and narrow stretch of water that separates Chesil Beach from mainland Dorset. The initial results were not promising, but on 23 January the bouncing bomb theory was at last proved credible. The size and cylindrical shape of the bomb was finally confirmed in late April. (IWM FLM2368)

ABOVE *A spherical prototype bomb of the type that was test-dropped from the Wellington into the Fleet. On the right is the central charge cylinder; on the left is one of two hollow end caps that made the bomb spherical.* (Cherwell Archives, Nuffield College)

LEFT *One of the prototype bouncing bombs is recovered from the Fleet.* (National Archives)

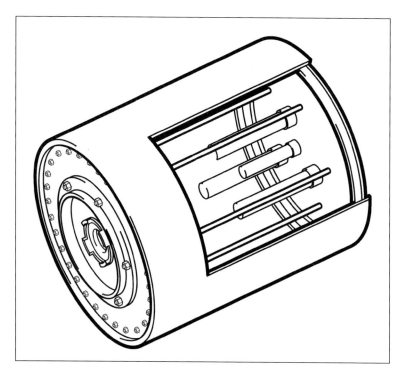

ABOVE *Cut-away illustration of the dam-busting weapon showing the three hydrostatic pistol detonators.*

RIGHT *In February 1943 the Chief of the Air Staff, Sir Charles Portal, ordered the immediate conversion of three Lancaster bombers for operational trials of 'Upkeep', as the bouncing bomb was now code-named. This view from beneath the Lancaster's nose, looking aft, shows the mine in place and protruding from the converted bomb bay.* (Crown Copyright)

from Lord Cherwell, the CRD and the Commander-in-Chief of Bomber Command, Sir Arthur Harris. It took the personal intervention of Sir Charles Portal, Chief of the Air Staff, to save the day. He overruled their concerns and decreed that the project should go ahead with the utmost urgency. On 26 February, orders were issued for the immediate conversion of three Avro Lancaster bombers for operational trials, a further twenty for conversion for operational use, and 150 bombs.

Vickers-Armstrongs at Barrow were contracted to manufacture the Upkeep mines, and Vickers also made the bomb-carrying and release mechanisms. Modification of the Lancasters was jointly undertaken by Avro and Vickers, with the latter using facilities at RAE Farnborough. Such was the urgency of the task that both contractors worked round-the-clock shifts, seven days a week.

The Upkeep bomb itself was in fact not a bomb but a cylindrical aerial mine, although it was invariably referred to as a bouncing bomb. Made out of metal some 3/8th inch thick, it measured about 60 inches in length by 50 inches in diameter and contained 6,600lb of Torpex explosive. Three hydrostatic pistols were set to detonate the explosive charge at a depth of 30ft and a fourth self-destruct

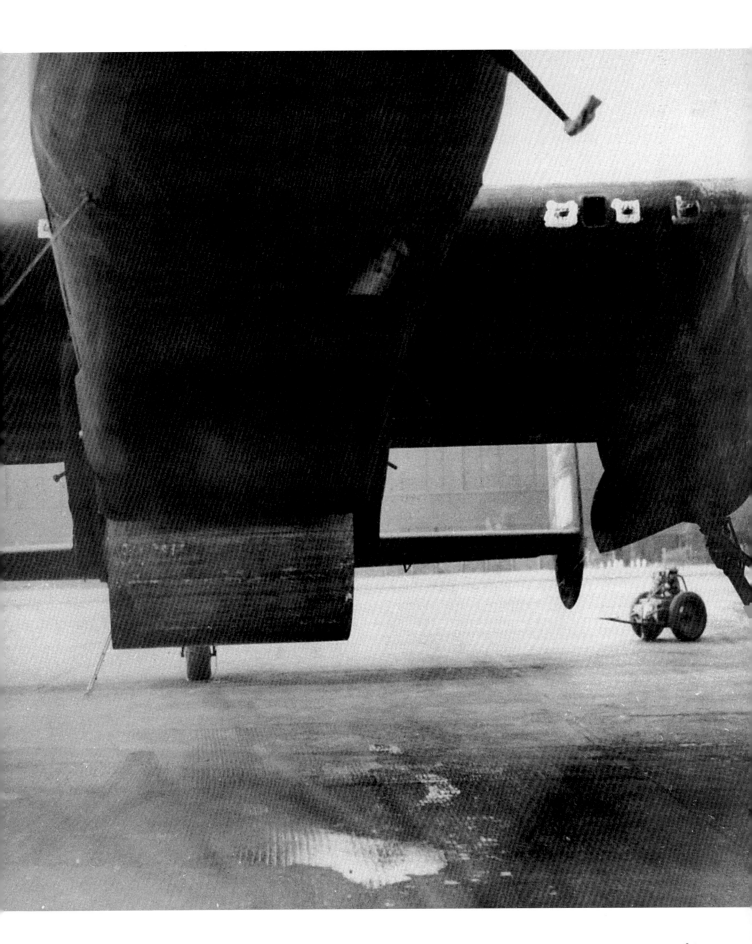

This well-known view of Guy Gibson's Lancaster, ED932/AJ-G, clearly shows the cut-away bomb bay with the Upkeep weapon mounted between the pair of side-swing callipers, and the belt drive to the weapon. (Crown Copyright)

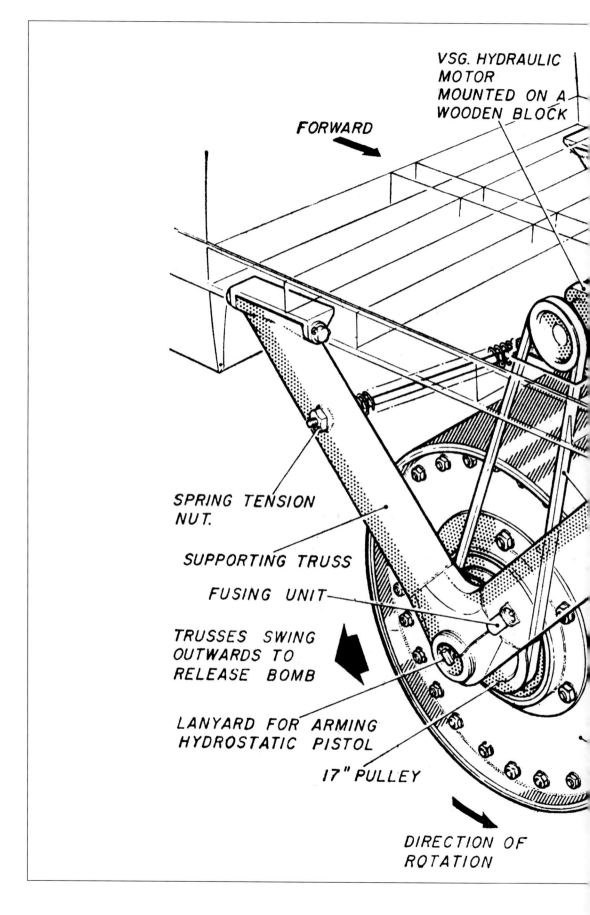

VSG. HYDRAULIC MOTOR MOUNTED ON A WOODEN BLOCK

FORWARD

SPRING TENSION NUT.

SUPPORTING TRUSS

FUSING UNIT

TRUSSES SWING OUTWARDS TO RELEASE BOMB

LANYARD FOR ARMING HYDROSTATIC PISTOL

17" PULLEY

DIRECTION OF ROTATION

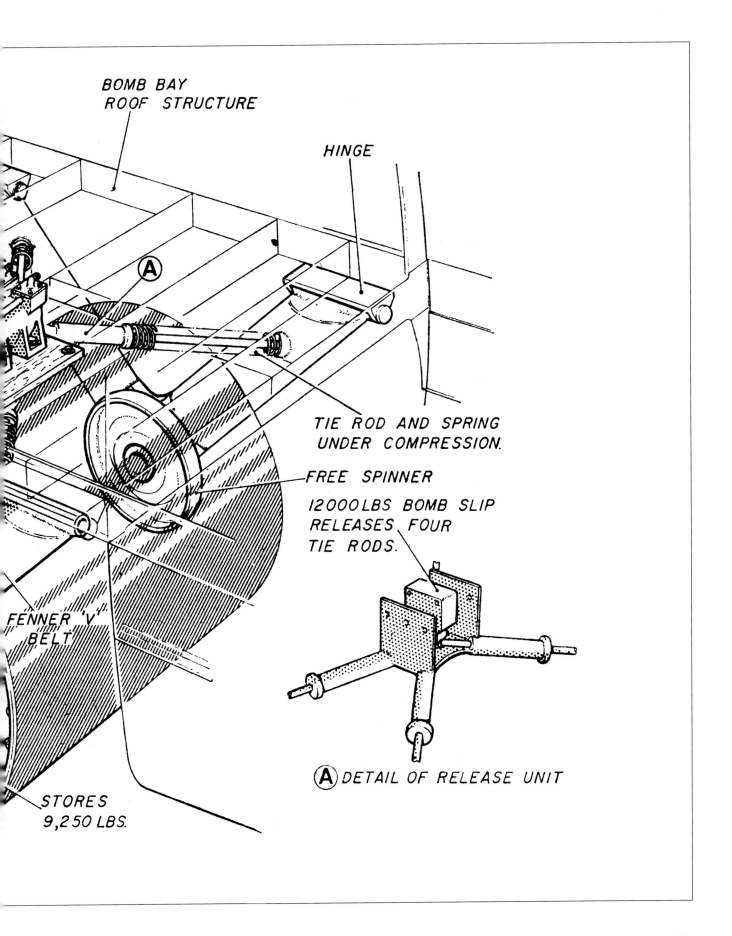

BOMB BAY
ROOF STRUCTURE

HINGE

(A)

TIE ROD AND SPRING
UNDER COMPRESSION.

FREE SPINNER

12000 LBS BOMB SLIP
RELEASES FOUR
TIE RODS.

FENNER 'V'
BELT

(A) DETAIL OF RELEASE UNIT

STORES
9,250 LBS.

pistol was timed to go off 90 seconds after the bomb had been released. Upkeep weighed in at 9,250lb and was carried in the belly of the specially modified Lancaster from which the bomb doors and mid-upper gun turret had been removed. Located in the aperture that had been the bomb bay, the bomb was mounted between two side-swing calliper arms, each of which was fitted with a 20in diameter disc. These corresponded to two circular tracks, one on each end of the cylindrical bomb, the back-spin being transmitted by friction generated between the driven discs and the circular tracks. Power for rotation was supplied by a Vickers Jassey Variable Speed Gear hydraulic motor driving a belt at an angle of 45 degrees, running in a groove on the driven disc in the starboard calliper arm. Hydraulic power originally intended for the Lancaster's mid-upper turret and the bomb bay doors was diverted to the hydraulic motor that was mounted in the floor of the fuselage in the facing of the bomb bay.

From his position just forward of the main spar, the wireless operator switched on the hydraulic motor that spun the bomb and he adjusted its rotation speed to the required 500rpm. Up in the cockpit beyond the navigator's curtained-off compartment, the pilot concentrated on flying straight and level while the flight engineer controlled the speed of the Lancaster on the approach run to the dam, and the navigator switched on the twin spotlights mounted on the underside of the aircraft. Looking out of the Perspex blister on the starboard side of the cockpit canopy, the navigator instructed the pilot on the necessary height corrections until the desired figure-of-eight alignment of the spotlights on the water below had been achieved.

When the bomb-aimer pressed the bomb-release button, powerful springs caused the calliper arms to spring outwards, thereby allowing the mine to drop free from the aircraft while at the same time arming the hydrostatic pistols.

The accurate delivery of Upkeep onto the target sounded difficult enough on paper, and the rigorous flying training programme devised for 617 Squadron's aircrews only served to emphasise this point. In fact, it became probably the longest, most intensive and most arduous bombing mission practice of the entire war.

BELOW *Illustration of the Type 464 Provisioning modifications made to the Lancaster in order for it to carry Upkeep.*

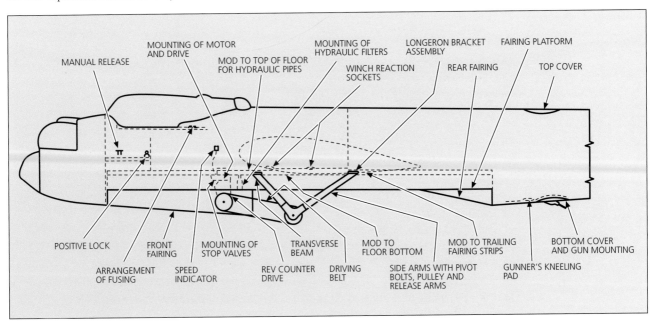

MANUAL RELEASE
MOUNTING OF MOTOR AND DRIVE
MOD TO TOP OF FLOOR FOR HYDRAULIC PIPES
MOUNTING OF HYDRAULIC FILTERS
WINCH REACTION SOCKETS
LONGERON BRACKET ASSEMBLY
FAIRING PLATFORM
REAR FAIRING
TOP COVER

POSITIVE LOCK
ARRANGEMENT OF FUSING
FRONT FAIRING
SPEED INDICATOR
MOUNTING OF STOP VALVES
REV COUNTER DRIVE
TRANSVERSE BEAM
DRIVING BELT
MOD TO FLOOR BOTTOM
SIDE ARMS WITH PIVOT BOLTS, PULLEY AND RELEASE ARMS
MOD TO TRAILING FAIRING STRIPS
GUNNER'S KNEELING PAD
BOTTOM COVER AND GUN MOUNTING

CHAPTER 3

Training for the Dams

Despite his vehement opposition to what he considered a crackpot invention by a mad scientist, Bomber Harris finally relented. On 15 March 1943 he ordered the formation of a special new bomber squadron. Harris's reluctant change of heart was due largely to pressure from the Chief of the Air Staff, Sir Charles Portal, who had been sufficiently impressed by the bomb trials at Chesil Beach and the model tests in the ship tanks at Teddington. Portal now wanted development of the bomb, modification of the aircraft and training of the Lancaster crews to proceed with the utmost urgency if the attack on the dams was to be mounted before the latest optimum date of 26 May. However, Harris

OPPOSITE
Wg Cdr Guy Gibson flies Lancaster ED932 at low level along the shoreline at Reculver in Kent, during bouncing bomb practice trials on 12 May 1943.
(IWM FLM 2352)

LEFT *In March 1943 Wg Cdr Guy Gibson was posted in to Scampton from 106 Squadron to command a new and secret Lancaster squadron, known enigmatically as Squadron X. Gibson is pictured (centre) when he was the commanding officer of 106 Squadron, flanked by his two flight commanders – Sqn Ldrs John Searby and Peter Ward-Hunt.*
(Crown Copyright)

warned Cochrane, the AOC of 5 Group, that the creation of the new squadron should not impact on the efforts of Bomber Command's Main Force squadrons, and that the planned attack on the Ruhr dams would not be its only task.

On 17 March the new squadron was officially formed. Known initially as Squadron X, it was to be commanded by a highly experienced 24-year-old wing commander named Guy Gibson. With two bomber and one night fighter tours under his belt already, and sporting the medal ribbons of two DSOs and two DFCs, Gibson had been the commanding officer of 106 Squadron at Syerston before his appointment to head up the new and top-secret Squadron X.

Bomber Command decreed that the crews for this new squadron were to be volunteers who had already completed at least one, and possibly two, bomber tours. Over the years a myth has grown up suggesting that all the men were young, highly experienced bomber veterans personally selected by Gibson. The reality is somewhat different, as the eminent aviation historian John Sweetman records in his book *The Dambusters Raid*: 'Not all the pilots were personally known to Gibson; aircrew ages ranged from twenty to thirty-two; the majority were not decorated (including six of the pilots); and far from having finished two operational tours some had not done one. Many who would fly to the German dams in May 1943 had completed fewer than ten operations against enemy targets, and some of the flight engineers were actually on their first.'

OPPOSITE *Kiwis at Scampton: the two New Zealanders on 617 Squadron were Flg Off L. Chambers (wireless operator in Mick Martin's crew) and Flt Lt Les Munro (captain of AJ-W). One of three flight commanders on the dams raid, Munro was forced to abort after his Lancaster was hit and damaged by flak over the Dutch island of Vlieland on the outward flight.* (IWM CH9937)

Squadron commander: Wg Cdr G.P. Gibson, DSO and Bar, DFC and Bar

Crew: Sgt J. Pulford DFM (FE), Plt Off T.H. Taerum DFC (N), Flt Lt E.G. Hutchison DFC and Bar (W/Op), Plt Off F.M. Spafford DFC (BA), Flt Sgt G.A. Deering DFC, RCAF (FG), Flt Lt R.A.D. Trevor-Roper DFC (RG)

Flt Lt L. J.V. Hopgood DFC and Bar (Captain)

Crew: Sgt C. Brennan (FE), Flg Off K. Earnshaw RCAF (N), Sgt J.W. Minchin (W/Op), Plt Off J.W. Fraser DFM (BA), Plt Off G.H.F.G. Gregory DFM (FG), Plt Off A.F. Burcher DFM, RAAF (RG)

Flt Lt H.B.M. Martin DFC (Captain)

Crew: Plt Off I. Whittaker (FE), Flt Lt J.F. Leggo DFC, RAAF (N), Flg Off L. Chambers RNZAF (W/Op), Flt Lt R.C. Hay DFC, RAAF (BA), Plt Off T.B. Foxlee DFM, RAAF (FG), Flt Sgt T.D. Simpson RAAF (RG)

Sqn Ldr H.M. Young DFC and Bar (Captain)

Crew: Sgt D.T. Horsfall (FE), Flt Sgt C.W. Roberts (N), Sgt L.W. Nichols (W/Op), Flg Off V.S. MacCausland RCAF (BA), Sgt G.A. Yeo (FG), Sgt W. Ibbotson (RG)

Flt Lt D.J. Maltby (Captain)

Crew: Sgt W. Hatton (FE), Sgt V. Nicholson (N), Sgt A.J.B. Stone (W/Op), Plt Off J. Fort (BA), Sgt V. Hill (FG), Sgt H.T. Simmonds (RG)

Flt Lt D. Shannon DFC, RAAF (Captain)

Crew: Sgt R.J. Henderson (FE), Flg Off D.R. Walker DFC, RCAF (N), Flg Off B. Goodale DFC (W/Op), Flt Sgt L.J. Sumpter (BA), Sgt B. Jagger (FG), Flg Off J. Buckley (RG)

Sqn Ldr H.E. Maudslay DFC (Captain)

Crew: Sgt J. Marriot (FE), Flg Off R.A. Urquhart (N), WO2 A.P. Cottam (W/Op), Plt Off M.J.D. Fuller (BA), Flg Off J. Tytherleigh (FG), Sgt N.R. Burrows (RG)

Flt Lt W. Astell DFC (Captain)

Crew: Sgt J. Kinnear (FE), Plt Off F.A. Wile (N), WO2 A. Garshowitz (W/Op), Flg Off D. Hopkinson (BA), Flt Sgt F.A. Garbas (FG), Sgt R. Bolitho (RG)

Plt Off L.G. Knight RAAF (Captain)

Crew: Sgt R.E. Grayston (FE), Flg Off H.S. Hobday (N), Flt Sgt R.G.T. Kellow (W/Op), Flg Off E.C. Johnson (BA), Sgt F.E. Sutherland (FG), Sgt H.E. O'Brien (RG)

Flt Lt R.N.G. Barlow DFC, RAAF (Captain)

Crew: Plt Off S.L. Whillis (FE), Flg Off P.S. Burgess (N), Flg Off C.R. Williams DFC, RAAF (W/Op), Plt Off A. Gillespie DFM (BA), Flg Off H.S. Glinz RCAF (FG), Sgt J.R.G. Liddell (RG)

Gibson and Sqn Ldr David Maltby, one of his flight commanders on 617 Squadron, pose for the camera in Gibson's office at Scampton. They are pictured after the dams raid on 22 July 1943. (IWM TR1122)

Flt Lt J.L. Munro (Captain)
Crew: Sgt F.E. Appleby (FE), Flg Off F.G. Rumbles (N), Sgt P.E. Pigeon (W/Op), Sgt J.H. Clay (BA), Sgt W. Howarth (FG), Flt Sgt H.A. Weeks (RG)

Plt Off V.W. Byers (Captain)
Crew: Sgt A.J. Taylor (FE), Flg Off J.H. Warner (N), Sgt J. Wilkinson (W/Op), Plt Off A.N. Whitaker (BA), Sgt C.McA. Jarvie (FG), Flt Sgt L. McDowell (RG)

Plt Off G. Rice (Captain)
Crew: Sgt E.C. Smith (FE), Flg Off R. MacFarlane (N), Sgt C.B. Gowrie (W/Op), Flt Sgt J.W. Thrasher (BA), Sgt T.W. Maynard (FG), Sgt S. Burns (RG)

Flt Lt J.C. McCarthy (Captain)
Crew: Sgt W. Radcliffe (FE), Flt Sgt D.A. MacLean (N), Sgt L. Eaton (W/Op), Sgt G.L. Johnson (BA), Sgt R. Batson (FG), Flg Off D. Rodger (RG)

Plt Off W. Ottley (Captain)
Crew: Sgt R. Marsden (FE), Flg Off J.K. Barrett (N), Sgt J. Guterman (W/Op), Flt Sgt T.B. Johnston (BA), Sgt F. Tees (FG), Sgt H.J. Strange (RG)

Plt Off L.J. Burpee (Captain)
Crew: Sgt G. Pegler (FE), Sgt T. Jaye (N), Plt Off L.G. Weller (W/Op), WO2 J.L. Arthur (BA), Sgt W.C.A. Long (FG), WO2 J.G. Brady (RG)

Flt Sgt K.W. Brown (Captain)
Crew: Sgt H.B. Feneron (FE), Sgt D.P. Heal (N), Sgt H.J. Hewstone (W/Op), Sgt S. Oancia (BA), Sgt D. Allatson (FG), Flt Sgt G.S. MacDonald (RG)

Plt Off W.C. Townsend (Captain)
Crew: Sgt D.J.D. Powell (FE), Plt Off C.L. Howard (N), Flt Sgt G.A. Chalmers (W/Op), Sgt C.E. Franklin (BA), Sgt D.E. Webb (FG), Sgt R.Wilkinson (RG)

Flt Sgt C.T. Anderson (Captain)
Crew: Sgt R.C. Patterson (FE), Sgt J.P. Nugent (N), Sgt W.D. Bickle (W/Op), Sgt G.J. Green (BA), Sgt E. Ewan (FG), Sgt A.W. Buck (RG)

Key: FE = flight engineer; N = navigator; W/Op = wireless operator; BA = bomb aimer; FG = front gunner; RG = rear gunner

RIGHT *Flt Lt David Shannon, pilot of AJ-L (left), with Flt Lt Dick Trevor-Roper, Gibson's rear gunner on the dams raid, and Sqn Ldr George Holden who was later to succeed Gibson as CO of 617 Squadron. (IWM TR1129)*

No. 106 Squadron provided three crew captains in Flt Lt John Hopgood, 21, from Seaford in Sussex, along with 20-year-old Flt Lt David Shannon DFC, RAAF, and Flt Sgt Lewis Burpee DFM, RCAF, aged 25, newly married and from Ottawa, Ontario.

Another 5 Group squadron, No. 57, provided three more pilots in the shape of Plt Off Geoff Rice, the 23-year-old Mancunian Flt Lt Bill Astell DFC, and Sqn Ldr Melvin 'Dinghy' Young DFC, who had sixty-five trips under his belt already. 'Dinghy' was so named because he had ditched twice in the North Sea. An Oxford rowing Blue, Young was Gibson's deputy as well as the commander of A Flight and was described by him as 'a big man, and a very efficient organiser. I was to find out later that he could drink a pint of beer faster than any other man I know.'

The B Flight commander was the ex-50 Squadron old-Etonian Sqn Ldr Henry Maudslay DFC, 21 years of age, from the Cotswold village of Broadway in Worcestershire. Also from 50 Squadron were Flt Lt Mick Martin DFC (a highly experienced Aussie pilot and an expert in low-level flying, serving in the RAF) and Plt Off Les Knight RAAF. In fact, 50 Squadron had been the breeding ground for some of the finest pilots and crews in Bomber Command, of which Guy Gibson and Mick Martin were among the three greatest bomber pilots of the Second World War.

No. 207 Squadron provided Plt Off Warner Ottley DFC, while 44 Squadron supplied 23-year-old Flt Sgt Ken Brown RCAF, from Moose Jaw, Saskatchewan. Also from Saskatchewan was Plt Off Vernon Byers RCAF, aged 32, from the town of Codette.

From 97 Squadron came Flt Lt David Maltby DFC – 'large and thoughtful, a fine pilot'; Flt Lt Les Munro RNZAF – 'a most charming fellow with an excellent operational record. He was one of those types who can always be relied on to do the right thing at the right moment.' And a 23-year-old American, Flt Lt Joe McCarthy DFC, RCAF. Born in St James, Long Island, McCarthy grew up in Brooklyn but when war broke out in Europe in 1939 he was desperate to see some action and so joined the RCAF, coming over to Britain to fly

ABOVE *Squadron X became 617 Squadron on 24 March 1943, although its badge was not officially approved until several months later.*

with Bomber Command in 1942. From St Kilda, Australia, via 61 Squadron, came 32-year-old Flt Lt Robert Barlow DFC, RAAF, and from 49 Squadron Sgt Cyril Anderson and Sgt Bill Townsend DFM.

Three other pilots were posted to 617 Squadron, but did not fly on the dams raid. They were 28-year-old Flt Lt Harold Wilson from Tottenham, north London, and Plt Off William Divall, 21, from Thornton Heath, Surrey (who had been brought in to replace Sgt Lovell and crew), both of whose crews were prevented from flying on Chastise due to sickness in their number. Later both captains were shot down by light flak and killed, as were their entire crews, as they attacked the Mittelland Canal on 15–16 September 1943. Flt Sgt G. Lanchester RCAF and his crew opted to leave the squadron after Gibson threatened to replace their navigator.

The 5 Group bomber airfield of Scampton

in Lincolnshire was chosen as the base for Squadron X. Situated 5 miles north of the city of Lincoln, Gibson had been stationed there earlier in the war flying Hampdens when he was with 83 Squadron. The new aircrews began to arrive at Scampton on 21 March, while all non-flying personnel were on the base by 27 March. Squadron X officially became 617 Squadron on the 24th and its adjutant, Flt Lt Harry Humphries, declared the new squadron ready to fly on the 25th.

On the 24th, Gibson travelled to see Barnes Wallis at Weybridge, where the scientist was hoping to give him a full briefing on the bomb and its intended targets. However, Gibson had not yet been cleared by Bomber Command to be given the full and specific details, so Wallis had to make do with outlining his ideas on the bomb and showing him a film of the bomb trials at Chesil Beach.

On the 27th, Cochrane's SASO, Gp Capt Harry Satterly, remembered by Gibson as 'a big blunt man who had the habit of getting things done quickly and well', issued Gibson with written orders that outlined the reason for the new squadron's existence – well, almost. The specific details of their intended target were still withheld, although Satterly's orders described how 617 Squadron would be required to attack a number of lightly defended special targets, necessitating low-level navigation over enemy territory in moonlight with a final approach to the target at 100ft at a precise speed of 240mph. He went on to say that aircraft would be despatched at ten-minute intervals to attack Target A and upon its successful destruction all subsequent aircraft would be diverted en route to fly to Target B, Target C and so on until the objectives of the operation had been achieved. While still not giving the game away, Satterly advised Gibson to see that his crews practised low-level flying over water, and on daylight training sorties to ensure that pilots and bomb aimers wore dark goggles to mimic moonlight conditions. To simulate night-flying conditions during daylight, blue celluloid was applied to the cockpit canopy and the gunners' turret Perspex, and amber-tinted interchangeable lenses were fitted to flying goggles. Helpfully, Satterly also told Gibson that there were nine lakes

in Wales and the Midlands that were suitable for flying practice. That same day, 617 was ready to commence its intensive flying training programme using ten standard Lancasters borrowed from another squadron.

On the 28th, Gibson took off from Scampton in a Lancaster accompanied by Flt Lt John Hopgood and Sqn Ldr Melvin 'Dinghy' Young and headed for the Derwent reservoir and dam in Derbyshire's Peak District to practise low flying at the height outlined in Satterly's briefing. During the hours of daylight Gibson found this a relatively easy task, but when he attempted to do the same at dusk it became clear just how dangerous the job was going to be: 'With the fog already beginning to fill up in the valley, cutting visibility down to about a mile or so, we tried again. This time it wasn't so good. The water, which had been blue by day, was now black – we nearly hit that black water.' The next day Gibson was

called to a meeting with Cochrane at 5 Group HQ in Grantham, where he was shown scale models of the Möhne and Sorpe dams and then told to visit Wallis again. It was on his next visit to Weybridge that Wallis and Mutt Summers explained to Gibson the construction of the Ruhr dams and their importance to German heavy industry.

Photo-reconnaissance of the dams was a vital ingredient to the success of Operation Chastise, as the attack on the dams was now code-named. It provided crucial information to Bomber Command's planning staff about the water levels in the dams' reservoirs as well as intelligence on anti-aircraft defences in the vicinity. Orders went out to RAF Benson in Oxfordshire on 25 January 1943 for one of its resident photo-reconnaissance units, 541 Squadron, to obtain coverage of the Möhne dam and its reservoir. On 7 February, the first in a series of nine PR sorties was flown

ABOVE *Training for the Ruhr dams raid over the Derwent dam and reservoir in the Derbyshire Peak District - a photograph taken during the making of* The Dam Busters *film in 1954.* (Garbett & Goulding Collection)

PREVIOUS SPREAD
Much of 617 Squadron's gruelling flying training programme in April and May 1943 was carried out over water using unmodified Lancasters borrowed from other squadrons. In addition to the coastal areas of the Wash and the Thames Estuary, nine inland lakes and reservoirs across England and Wales were used by day and night for low-flying and bombing practice. In this wonderfully evocative photograph, the Battle of Britain Memorial Flight's (BBMF) Lancaster, PA474, is pictured flying over the English coast. (Richard Winslade)

RIGHT *The Derwent dam and reservoir in Derbyshire's Peak District was used to hone 617's low-flying and precision-bombing skills. Its twin towers were useful in testing the principle of the simple Dann bombsight that was specially invented for the purposes of Upkeep. Pictured here, on 16 May 1988, the BBMF's Lancaster overflies the Derwent dam to mark the 45th anniversary of the dams raid. For 6 miles around, more than 50,000 people thronged to witness the spectacle.* (Atlantic Syndication)

RIGHT *From January 1943 a series of photo-reconnaissance sorties were flown over the Ruhr dams. This photograph of the Möhne was taken on 3 April 1943 from a Spitfire PRXI of 541 Squadron flown by Flg Off J.R. Brew.* (Crown Copyright)

RIGHT *One of the PRU's aims was to bring back photographs of high enough quality for skilled model makers to build three-dimensional scale models of the dams. This is a model of the Sorpe dam.* (IWM MH3780)

to the Möhne by a Spitfire of 541 Squadron. The weather conditions over western Germany were not ideal for photography and it was not until the seventh attempt on the 19th that useful material was brought back. Two more sorties were deemed necessary to provide photographs of good enough quality to enable accurate scale models of the dam and its reservoir to be built for aircrew briefing purposes. Periodically, in the weeks that followed, the dam was photographed by 541 and 542 Squadrons to provide additional information about the dam itself and changes in the water level and defences.

On 5 April Bomber Command made a further request for photo-reconnaissance coverage, only this time to include the Eder and Sorpe dams. The final reconnaissance

was completed by 15 May and the latest photographs and interpretations were ready by mid-afternoon that same day. Detailed scale models were built of both dams and their hinterlands to aid crews at their operational briefing. For the most part, photographic sorties to the dams were flown by the same pilots each time. This was to familiarise them with the dams and their surrounding landscapes, so that when they flew the post-raid reconnaissance sorties they would be able to accurately observe the changes brought about by the flooding.

Throughout April, when weather conditions permitted, the crews of 617 Squadron carried out intensive flying training on a daily basis, and by the end of that month Gibson was able to report that all his crews could navigate at

low level by night, fly safely over water at a height of 150ft and bomb accurately with the aid of a special bombsight. In *Enemy Coast Ahead*, he remarked:

'The boys had begun to get good at their flying, and now I knew where and what the targets were we could plan a route similar to the one which would actually be used over Germany. This meant flying a lot over lakes, but the excuse was always the same: they were good landmarks and a good check on navigation. As we would have to fly to Germany at tree-level height, keeping to track was most important, and it meant navigation to the yard.'

From 5 May, all training was undertaken at the Eyebrook reservoir (also referred to as

Uppingham Lake), where ten Lancasters at a time were to practise flying at 60ft above the water. In addition to this, cross-country flying exercises were still undertaken to further improve navigational skills that would prove invaluable when it came to the real operation. The Abberton reservoir near Colchester (also known as Colchester Lake) and Lake Bala in North Wales were also used for low-level flying and bombing practice.

In the days that followed, the skills of 617's nineteen bomber crews were honed to a high degree of operational capability – pilots could fly at 60ft over water while maintaining an air speed of 210mph; with the aid of Gee and careful map reading, navigators could find their way around the countryside with precision

at low level in the dark; bomb-aimers had refined their techniques with practice bombs to achieve an average error of 117ft; and gunners had harmonised their sights and sharpened their gunnery skills to make them potent adversaries for enemy night fighters and flak gunners.

The crews themselves might have been trained and ready, but two important technical matters could make or break all their hard work – an effective bombsight with which to accurately aim the bombs, and a means of precisely calculating the height of an aircraft above the reservoirs.

First of all, because of the extreme low level at which the bombs were to be dropped, no bombsight then in use by the RAF could do the job. Surprisingly, the solution was very simple and effective. A hand-held wooden sight was designed by Wg Cdr C.L. Dann at the A&AEE Boscombe Down, for use by the bomb aimers of 617 Squadron. In order to achieve an accurate release point for the Upkeep weapon, Dann used calculations based on the width between the sluice towers of the Möhne dam to make a simple triangular wooden sight. With a sighting peephole at the apex and two nails at the extremities of the base, the bomb aimer held the sight by a wooden handle attached to the underside of the apex and looked through the peephole. On the bombing run, when the twin towers of the dam coincided with the two nails the bomb aimer pressed the bomb release mechanism. A trial flight over the Derwent dam proved the effectiveness of the device and Barnes Wallis worked out the relevant sighting data for each dam to be attacked.

However, the Dann sight had its drawbacks. Buffeting of the aircraft at low level by thermals meant that it was nearly impossible for a bomb aimer to hold a sight steady with both hands and still maintain his balance in the bomb-aiming compartment. Some bomb aimers dispensed with the Dann sight altogether and experimented with their own sighting devices, which included chinagraph pencil marks on the clear vision panel and lengths of string attached to screws each side of the panel to create a large triangle. Lying prone on the floor of the aircraft supported by their forearms, some bomb aimers saw this

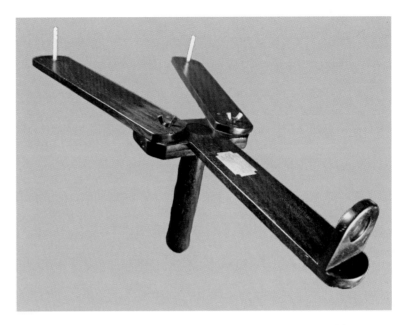

ABOVE *An original example of the hand-held wooden Dann sight as used by 617 Squadron's bomb aimers on the dams raid.* (David Worrow)

as a more stable position to adopt during the bombing run.

The conundrum of how to maintain a specific height at low level over water and in the dark taxed the greatest brains at the MAP and at RAE Farnborough. Gibson was at a loss to find an effective way of judging the right height, and in the end it was the gentle, kindly figure of Ben Lockspeiser, civilian Director of Scientific Research at MAP, who solved the riddle. Trials carried out in 1942 on Lockheed Hudsons of Coastal Command had used twin spotlights to assist in night attacks on submarines in shallow water, but without success – the twin lights had converged beneath the rough surface of the water. Lockspeiser successfully argued that on the calm water of an inland lake this would not be a problem, and trials were quickly set up at Farnborough. After a series of tests it was decided that the optimum positioning for the twin Aldis lamps on a Lancaster would be one in the portside of the nose, aft of the bomb aimer's clear vision panel, and the second in the rear of the bomb bay. Both lamps were angled to starboard and when the aircraft was flying at the prescribed 150ft (later reduced to 60ft) above the water, the twin beams would converge to form a figure of eight on the water beneath and just forward of the leading edge of the starboard wing. This enabled the navigator to check the height from the Perspex blister on the starboard side of the cockpit.

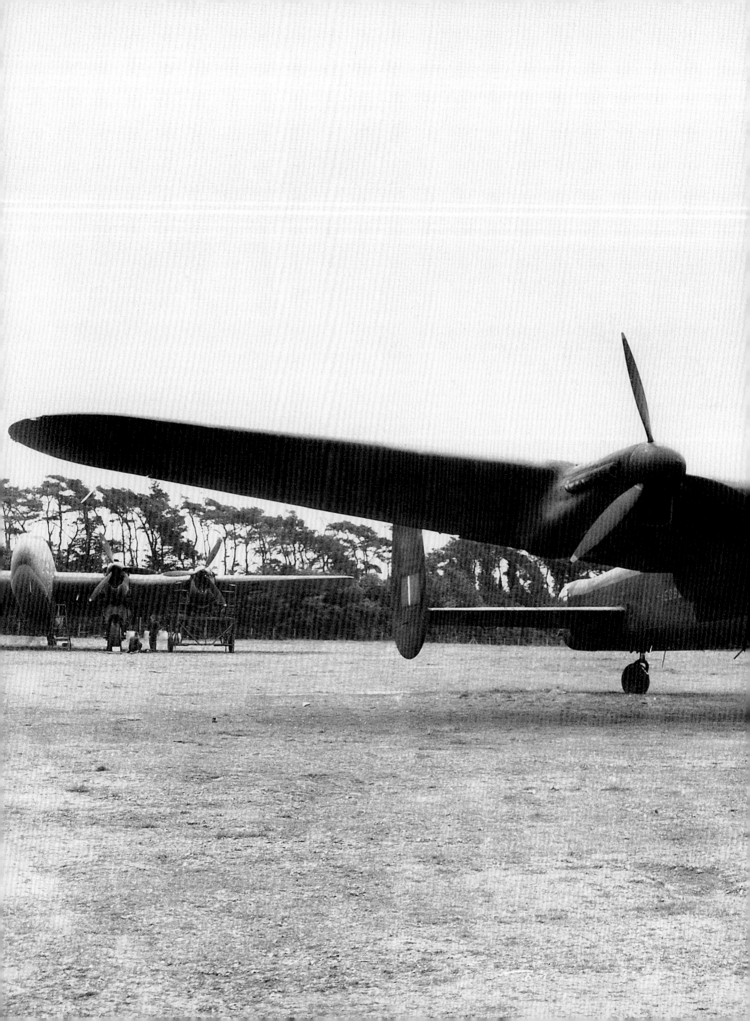

PREVIOUS SPREAD *By early May, 617 Squadron had received 18 modified Type 464 Provisioning Lancasters. This is ED825 that was used at A&AEE Boscombe Down for handling trials of the fully loaded bomber. It was flown by Flt Lt Joe McCarthy on Chastise. The side-swing callipers and drive belt can be clearly seen in this photograph. (IWM ATP11384B)*

INSET *ED817 took part in the Upkeep dropping trials at Reculver on 20 April. Although the aircraft did not fly on the actual dams raid, this photograph gives a good indication of how much the bomb bay was remodelled on the Type 464 Provisioning Lancasters. (Bruce Robertson collection)*

RIGHT *This view shows to good advantage the absence of a dorsal turret and the cut-away bomb bay on McCarthy's Lancaster, ED825. (Crown Copyright)*

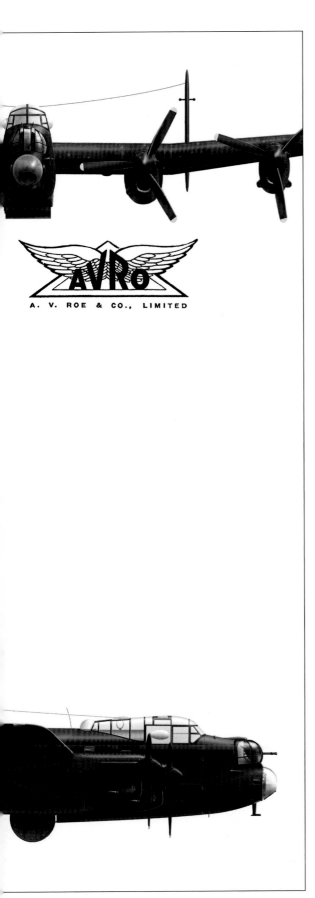

A. V. ROE & CO., LIMITED

It was not until 8 April that the first of the modified Lancasters reached the squadron. By the end of the month thirteen of the Type 464 Provisioning aircraft had arrived, which meant that the borrowed unmodified Lancasters, used until then for training purposes, could be returned to their owner squadrons. However, because of the great haste in which the modifications had been carried out by the contractors, not everything had been completed on time. Therefore some of the modifications that should have been undertaken by Avro were carried out at Scampton by the base engineering staff, assisted by supervisors from Avro, RAE and MAP. By early May, eighteen modified Lancasters had been received and fitted with VHF radios; twenty Upkeep weapons had also arrived and were ready for balancing (to ensure they rotated true and did not oscillate); practice Upkeeps had been delivered and were being prepared for crews to use in a night trial off Reculver on the north Kent coast.

On the night of 6–7 May, the squadron flew a full exercise over the Eyebrook, Abberton and Howden reservoirs, Derwent dam, Wainfleet and the Wash, simulating the attack pattern that had been planned for the actual operations against the Möhne, Eder and Sorpe dams. Three formations, each of three aircraft, carried out practice attacks on the reservoirs, and the Derwent dam, while the rest of the squadron, the mobile reserve, practised bombing over the Wash with the aid of their twin Aldis spotlights.

On 10 May Satterly wrote to Gp Capt John Whitworth at Scampton with the first draft order for the forthcoming operation, which the station commander used as a discussion document with Gibson. It was resolved that the attack should be mounted by twenty Lancasters, with three sections of three aircraft taking off at ten-minute intervals, followed by individual aircraft taking off at three-minute intervals. Aircraft were to cross the North Sea at 60ft and maintain this low level across the continent, with the formation leader climbing to 500ft en route to check landmarks, and, when 10 miles from the target, climbing to between 1,000 and 1,500ft. Targets were designated A, B and C, corresponding to the Möhne, Eder and Sorpe dams. The leader

LEFT *Avro Lancaster B Mk III (Type 464 Provisioning).* (Paul Couper/www. paulcouper.co.uk)

ABOVE *Without its mid-upper turret and bomb bay doors, a modified Lancaster drops a full-size Upkeep in the sea on the north Kent coast at Reculver Bay during tests in May 1943. The first modified Lancasters reached 617 Squadron on 8 April and the Upkeep trials were switched from Chesil Beach to Reculver on the 13th because the latter offered better security and easier recovery of the dropped weapons for examination.* (IWM FLM2340)

RIGHT *People living near the isolated 4-mile-long Lake Bala in North Wales were frightened out of their wits as 617's Lancasters swept low over the lake at night on practice sorties.* (Author)

would make an immediate assault on target A, and when he had completed his attack he would wait 90 seconds before calling in the second aircraft to attack, followed by the third. By this time the second formation would have arrived and the procedure would be repeated, with the third formation following on. Each aircraft would fire a red flare over the dam after dropping its mine as a safety precaution for the next aircraft in line to attack. When target A had been destroyed, aircraft would divert to B, where they would follow the same assault pattern, while simultaneously target C would be hit by five Lancasters as a distraction from the attacks under way on targets A and B. After completing their attacks, individual crews were to make their own way home at low level and high speed.

During April and early May, test pilots 'Sam' Brown (Avro) and Sqn Ldr M.V. Longbottom (on secondment from the RAF to Vickers), and

Vickers' flight-test observer Bob Handasyde carried out a series of trial weapon drops in the sea off Reculver, between Herne Bay and Birchington. As a test area it offered better security than Chesil Beach in Dorset, and it also allowed easier recovery of the dropped weapons for examination. The first of several trials at this new test location took place on 13 April using a converted Wellington bomber and reduced size practice spheres. Two high-speed cine cameras were used to record the results and an observer marked on a Perspex screen the number of bounces made by each bomb. The first sphere to be dropped in this series of tests was released from a height of 250ft and broke up on hitting the sea; the second, although dropped from only 50ft, suffered some damage but succeeded in bouncing across the surface of the water for some distance. Three more spheres were test-dropped on 18 April, another on the 21st and one more on the 22nd.

BELOW *Watched by a small group of steely-nerved observers, including Gibson and Wallis, an inert Upkeep filled with concrete bounces off the sea and bowls up the beach at Reculver, at some time between 11 and 14 May 1943. (IWM FLM2343)*

THIS SPREAD *This fascinating four-picture sequence shows a modified Lancaster making a trial drop of an Upkeep weapon. Flying at probably not more than 40ft above the sea, its rear fuselage and tail plane are engulfed by the great plume of water made by the bomb as it makes its first bounce. Although the Lancaster emerges largely intact, the tail plane appears to have suffered damage and it may have lost the tail wheel. ED921 flown by Les Munro, and ED933, flown by Henry Maudslay, were both damaged during the trials at Reculver due to flying below the prescribed height of 60ft. These important photographs are movie stills taken from a film that was only rediscovered in 1993, deep in the archives of TRL Ltd (formerly the Road Research Laboratory). (IWM FLM 2360/1/2/3)*

These superb head-on shots - once again movie stills - were probably taken on 11 May 1943 and capture the moment as Guy Gibson, having just released his Upkeep weapon over the Reculver range, pilots ED932, G for George, towards the camera and then thunders overhead with the Lancaster's four Merlins at full chat. Operation Chastise is less than a week away.
(IWM FLM2348/2353)

On 28 April further dropping trials were flown and from their results the final shape and size of the bouncing bomb was determined as a cylinder and not a sphere. Among the trial observers on this occasion were Barnes Wallis, accompanied by Guy Gibson.

On 1 May Longbottom dropped the first full-size Upkeep cylinder at Reculver. On the 11th, three of the new Type 464 Provisioning Lancasters of 617 Squadron for the first time

dropped inert Upkeeps at Reculver, and the next day further aircraft from the squadron carried out more trial drops. Using dummy towers on the promenade as their targets, the Upkeep weapons bounced across the surface of the sea and bowled up the beach. These practice attacks continued for the next two days, but two precious aircraft were damaged in the process, one beyond repair. The tail plane of ED921, flown by Les Munro, was

damaged due to the practice Upkeep being dropped from below the prescribed 60ft, but happily the Lancaster was repairable in time for the operation itself. However, ED933, flown by Henry Maudslay, was badly damaged, and despite the best efforts of the workshop staff at Scampton, it was scrubbed from the battle order on the 16th. On the 13th, the only fully armed live Upkeep mine to be spun and dropped before the operation was released from a Lancaster in a trial 5 miles off the Kent coast at Broadstairs. A camera crew located at the North Foreland captured on film the resulting explosion, which raised a plume of water hundreds of feet into the air.

On the evening of the 14th, the nineteen specially modified Type 464 Provisioning Lancasters now available to the squadron flew their last exercise together before Operation Chastise. The following day, last-minute checks and adjustments were made to the weapon and its release mechanism after a second live Upkeep was dropped off Broadstairs, but this time without being spun.

The stage was now set for the big 'op', but as yet none of the crews knew the identity of their intended target. Speculation was rife, with the favourite being a low-level attack on the German battleship *Tirpitz*, but soon all would be revealed.

ABOVE *On 13 May the only fully armed live Upkeep to be spun and dropped before Chastise was released from a Lancaster in a trial 5 miles off the Kent coast at Broadstairs.* (IWM FLM2365)

BELOW *In April 1975 four inert concrete-filled Upkeeps were recovered from the mud some 200yds offshore from Reculver. A USAF Sikorsky HH53 'Jolly Green Giant' helicopter was used to lift the bombs on to dry land.*

CHAPTER 4

Operation Chastise

'Operation Chastise. Immediate attack of targets X, Y and Z approved. Execute at first suitable opportunity.' With this top-secret message to HQ Bomber Command from the office of the Chief of the Air Staff on 15 May, the momentous decision to proceed with the attack on the Ruhr dams was taken. A staff car containing Cochrane was soon despatched from 5 Group HQ to drive the short distance to Scampton, where the AOC met with Whitworth and Gibson to inform them that the operation was on for the next day, 16 May. That evening, Gibson and Wallis briefed the two flight commanders, Dinghy Young and Henry

RIGHT *Guy Gibson in contemplative mood. At the time of Chastise he was a 24-year-old veteran pilot, having already completed 170 flying sorties as a bomber and night fighter pilot. He is pictured here wearing a non-regulation captured German Schwimmweste, the Luftwaffe equivalent of the RAF's Mae West. These gas-inflated life vests were highly prized among RAF aircrew. (IWM CH11047)*

OVERLEAF *Gibson with four of his crew, photographed after the dams raid. Fred Spafford (bomb aimer), Bob Hutchison (wireless operator), George Deering (front gunner), and Torger Taerum (navigator). (IWM TR1127)*

Maudslay, as well as John Hopgood (Gibson's deputy leader for the attack on the Möhne) and Bob Hay (the bombing leader), on the operation that was scheduled for the following night. After the informal briefing, Whitworth broke the sad news to Gibson that his faithful black Labrador companion, Nigger, had been killed in a road accident outside the camp's main gate. Some feared this was a bad omen for the forthcoming operation.

In the early afternoon of 16 May, Scampton's tannoy system crackled into life. 'All crews of No. 617 Squadron to report to the briefing room immediately.' The great secret was finally shared when Gibson and Wallis revealed details of the targets to 617's aircrew at a first briefing for the squadron's pilots and navigators, bomb aimers and gunners. Meanwhile, 5 Group's chief signals officer, Wg Cdr Dunn, briefed the wireless operators on the special signals requirements for the night ahead. Crews also had the opportunity to study reconnaissance photographs of their targets as well as the carefully made scale models of the Möhne and Sorpe dams, built by the RAF Central Interpretation Unit's model section in Danesfield House at Medmenham, in the Thames Valley.

In the hangars and out on the dispersals the ground crews struggled to ensure that every aircraft was serviceable and ready for war. Petrol bowsers pumped 10,800lbs of 100 octane fuel into each aircraft's six self-sealing tanks; teams of armourers toiled to feed the front and rear turrets with 18,000 and 12,000 rounds of tracer ammunition respectively. However, Lancaster ED933, which had been damaged by Maudslay during practice on 13 May, was declared beyond repair in time for the operation, leaving only nineteen of the modified Lancasters available. Sickness meant that the crews of Plt Off William Divall and Flt Lt Harold Wilson who had been rostered for the operation would not be flying after all. This was fortuitous, since there would have been insufficient aircraft available for them.

The weather had been unseasonably hot that day, and the air was still very warm when the final and formal briefing for all aircrew was held at 18.00hrs in the upstairs briefing room at Scampton. When the platform party

of Gibson, Wallis, Gp Capt Whitworth and Air Vice-Marshal Cochrane swept in and made their way to the front of the briefing room, the crews quickly realised the significance of the operation they were soon to be called upon to fly. Gibson told the gathered crews to sit down, and drawing aside the blackout curtain that covered the large map of Germany on the wall, he boldly announced to the expectant audience that their target for that night was the great dams of western Germany. Wallis was then introduced and the softly spoken, white-haired scientist ran through again what he had said on 15 May, and indeed earlier that day. He explained why the dams had been chosen for attack and outlined some of the problems he had encountered in developing the special weapon they would be using later that night. Once Wallis had finished his briefing, the AOC stood up and gave the crews a pep talk. He swore them to secrecy about the details of the weapon and finished with the remark, 'Now you are off on a raid that will do a tremendous amount of damage. It will become historic.' His words were prophetic.

When Cochrane stood down from the platform, Gibson rose to run through the operational details once again. The first wave comprising three sections of three aircraft consisted of Gibson, Hopgood, Martin, Young, Astell, Maltby, Maudslay, Knight and Shannon. They would take off at ten-minute intervals and fly the southern route from Scampton, across the North Sea to make landfall over the Scheldt estuary, between Noord Beveland and Schouwen, and thence to the Möhne dam (Target X), where they were to press home their attack until the dam had definitely been breached. Once the Möhne had been breached, the remaining aircraft of the first wave that were still carrying mines would divert to the Eder dam (Target Y), where the same procedure would be followed until that dam had also been breached. When the Möhne and the Eder had both been breached, those aircraft still with mines would fly on to the Sorpe dam (Target Z). In the meantime, the second wave of five Lancasters, comprising McCarthy, Byers, Barlow, Rice and Munro, would take off singly and fly the northern route across the North Sea to the Dutch island of Vlieland before turning

south-east over the Zuider Zee (Ijsselmeer) to join the same route as the first wave, at a point north-west of the German town of Wesel. The third wave, consisting of five aircraft, captained by Townsend, Anderson, Brown, Ottley and Burpee, considered as a 'mobile reserve', would take off two and a half hours later and fly the same southern route as the first wave. Its brief was to attack the 'last resort' targets of the Lister (Target D), Ennepe (Target E), and Diemel (Target F) dams.

Aircraft were to cross England at 1,500ft before descending to low level to cross the North Sea. At this point they were to set their altimeters to 60ft and maintain this low level all the way to the target. They were expected to fly at the same low level on the way home, at least until they had left the enemy coast behind. Low-level flying was vital to avoid the unwelcome attentions of German radar, flak and night fighters.

As a final summary of what was expected that night, Gibson outlined the routes to be followed to and from the targets, and confirmed timings, code words and other operational details for the three waves of aircraft. The briefing ended at 19.30hrs and crews made their way to their respective messes for the traditional pre-op meal of bacon and eggs.

In the meantime, Bomber Command HQ had made contact with RAF Benson to inform them of the exact time of the attack, so that PR coverage of the results could be obtained as early as possible the next morning by putting an aircraft over the targets soon after first light.

An entry written in the squadron record book by Flt Lt Harry Humphries, 617's adjutant, conveys something of the special mood in the air at Scampton in the hours before take-off:

'This was Der Tag for 617 Squadron. Hardly a soul with the exception of the crews knew the target. Very few people outside the squadron knew we were operating – not even the WAAFs. From eight o'clock onwards the scenes outside the crew rooms were something to be remembered. It was not like an ordinary operational scene, all the crews on this occasion being aware of the terrific task confronting them. Most of them wore expressions varying from the "don't care a damn" to the grim and determined. On the whole I think it appeared rather reminiscent of a crusade.'

In the locker rooms the crews changed into their flying kit. Valuables were handed in for safekeeping and escape kits collected. Sandwiches and flasks of coffee for the return journey, together with slabs of Fry's Sandwich chocolate and barley sugar sweets, were handed out to each man from wrappings of newspaper. Outside the locker room the buses arrived to take the crews on the bumpy ride to their aircraft dispersed around the airfield. A corporal stood at the open door shouting out the letters by which each aircraft was known. As space became available on a bus for that aircraft's crew, they climbed on board and were driven out to their waiting Lancaster.

At 21.10hrs Gibson's wireless operator, Flt Lt Bob Hutchison, fired a red Very light into the cloudless evening sky, signalling that all aircraft in the first and second waves should start engines. Looking out of the cockpit window to the ground below, Gibson's flight engineer, Sgt John Pulford, called back to his skipper that the ground crew were ready to start the port inner. Switching on the ignition and booster coil, Pulford pressed the starter button on the cockpit instrument panel and the first of the four 1,480hp Rolls-Royce Merlin 28 engines coughed, spluttered and finally burst into life. The same procedure was repeated by fourteen aircraft until the air became alive with the sound of fifty-six Merlin engines being warmed up to operating temperature.

The Lancasters taxied in stately progress around the airfield perimeter track to the take-off point. Because they were flying the longer northerly route, the aircraft from the second wave were the first to take off. At 21.28hrs

LEFT *With minutes to go before boarding G for George, Bob Hutchison exchanges a few words with Gibson, who is fastening his parachute harness.* (IWM CH9682)

OVERLEAF *Freezing a moment in time, this historic photograph captures Gibson and his crew as they hesitate briefly for the camera before climbing inside G for George on the evening of 16 May. Only four of the nine photographs taken before and after the raid were passed by the censor for publication, such was the security surrounding Chastise. From left to right: Trevor-Roper, Pulford, Deering, Spafford, Hutchison, Gibson and Taerum.* (IWM CH18005)

Operation Chastise got under way as the first aircraft of the second wave, piloted by Flt Lt Bob Barlow, lumbered off Scampton's grass runway, followed at one-minute intervals by the remaining four aircraft. However, a coolant leak in AJ-Q forced Flt Lt Joe McCarthy to rapidly switch his crew to the reserve aircraft, AJ-T, but this too was unserviceable due to the absence of the compass deviation card. Without this, accurate flying along the carefully charted route to the dams would be impossible. Fortunately, the squadron's senior NCO, Flt Sgt G.E. 'Chiefy' Powell, had met the furious McCarthy on his way to the instrument section and had miraculously located the missing card. AJ-T was now ready for business and took off twenty minutes late, behind the rest of the second-wave aircraft that were already heading into the gathering dusk, eastwards across the North Sea.

At 21.39hrs the green Aldis light winked through the twilight from the chequered flare-path caravan, giving take-off clearance to Gibson. The four Merlin engines of AJ-G were run up against the wheel brakes, and with a hiss of compressed air the brakes were released, the throttles were advanced and the Lancaster lurched forward on its take-off run. The aircraft of Hopgood (AJ-M) and Martin (AJ-P) joined G for George on either side. They were soon followed by Young (AJ-A), Maltby (AJ-J) and Shannon (AJ-L) at 21.47hrs, and Maudslay (AJ-Z), Astell (AJ-B) and Knight (AJ-N) at 21.59hrs.

The first wave was now airborne and Gibson led it by the fast fading light of the setting sun to the Wash and on towards the south-east, crossing out over the English coast at Southwold. Flying low across the North Sea to escape detection by German radar, strict radio silence was observed. With the first traces of moonlight dancing along a narrow silver pathway across the dark waters skimming by close beneath their wings, Gibson and the first wave made landfall on the Dutch coast. They were a few miles further south than planned, over the heavily defended island of Walcheren, but quickly corrected their course towards Roosendaal. Looking around him, Gibson noticed with satisfaction that Hopgood and Martin were still there and flying in perfect formation alongside him.

As luck would have it, they had taken the enemy defences by surprise and no flak rose to greet them. Gibson recalls in *Enemy Coast Ahead* that they were flying very low. 'We were flying so low that more than once Spam [Spafford] yelled at me to pull up quickly to avoid high-tension wires and tall trees.' At Roosendaal, a further course change saw them head almost due east to follow the glistening ribbon of the Wilhelmina Canal that took them between the Luftwaffe night fighter bases at Gilze Rijen and Eindhoven. Some distance further on, at the town of Beek, the canal intersected with another waterway, the Zuid Willemsvaart, in a T-junction which was the landmark for the formation to turn towards the River Rhine and the German frontier. Realising they were off course again, in fact some 6 miles too far to the south, Gibson banked sharply to port and flew up the Rhine in the direction of Rees before turning east towards Ahsen and the cluster of small lakes at Dulmen.

Over the Rhine the formation received its first dose of enemy fire from flak gunners on river barges, whose rounds were eagerly returned by the Lancasters' vigilant gunners. In the Borken area a heavy concentration of flak and searchlights caused difficulties, while north-west of Dorsten proved to be another hot spot, with all three lead aircraft caught in the blinding glare of probing searchlights. Thundering across the German countryside at tree-top height, more trouble awaited as the first wave flew towards Dulmen, where light flak damaged the port wing of Hopgood's AJ-M. This caused Gibson to break radio silence and call up 5 Group headquarters with a flak warning for the aircraft that were following. Flying north of the notorious town of Hamm with its heavily defended railway marshalling yards, Gibson's first flight of three Lancasters approached its final major turning point at Ahlen, from where it flew due south in the velvet darkness between the sleeping towns of Werl and Soest towards the distant Ruhr hills. The first flight arrived over the Möhne dam at 00.20hrs. 'As we came over the hill,' wrote Gibson, 'we saw the Möhne Lake. Then we saw the dam itself. In that light it looked squat and heavy and unconquerable.'

Some 6 minutes behind Gibson was the second flight of three Lancasters led by Sqn Ldr Dinghy Young in AJ-A, with Maltby (AJ-J) and Shannon (AJ-L), who reached the Möhne at 00.26hrs. They too had encountered flak en route, but it was the third flight of the first wave led by Sqn Ldr Henry Maudslay in AJ-Z that suffered the first fatality of the night. Shortly after crossing into Germany from Holland, Astell's Lancaster (AJ-B) was flying at the prescribed low level, but appeared to hesitate at a course change. Astell failed to turn with Maudslay and Knight, and lagged behind. Near the village of Marbeck, AJ-B flew into an electricity pylon, whereupon the aircraft erupted into a ball of flame and staggered on a little further before crashing in a field. Several minutes later the mine exploded with devastating consequences. All seven crew died.

To give the attacking aircraft as much protection as possible from defensive flak on and around the dam wall itself, the Lancasters were to dive over the Körbecke road bridge that spanned the Möhne lake. Each aircraft would then fly along the lake before turning and climbing a little to cross over the wooded Hever promontory, then dropping down to the prescribed attack height again on the final one-mile run-in to the dam. This still left the aircraft to adjust their height and speed on the most crucial phase of their bombing run, vulnerable to the withering gunfire from enemy flak positions.

Gibson flew over the Möhne dam in a dummy run to investigate the defences, braving the concentrated fire of some twelve light flak guns situated on the sluice towers, dam wall and in the fields that surrounded the dam. He recalls: 'It was light flak, mostly green, yellow and red, and the colours of the tracer reflected upon the face of the water in the lake. The reflections on the dead calm of the black water made it seem there was twice as much as there really was.' Pleased with what he had observed and unscathed by the attentions of the German gunners, Gibson called up the five other aircraft and prepared them to commence their individual attack runs on his command. 'Hello, all Cooler aircraft. I am going to attack. Stand by to come in to attack in your order when I tell you.'

OVERLEAF Map showing the routes to and from the targets, with approximate positions of aircraft losses and aborted sorties. (Martin Latham)

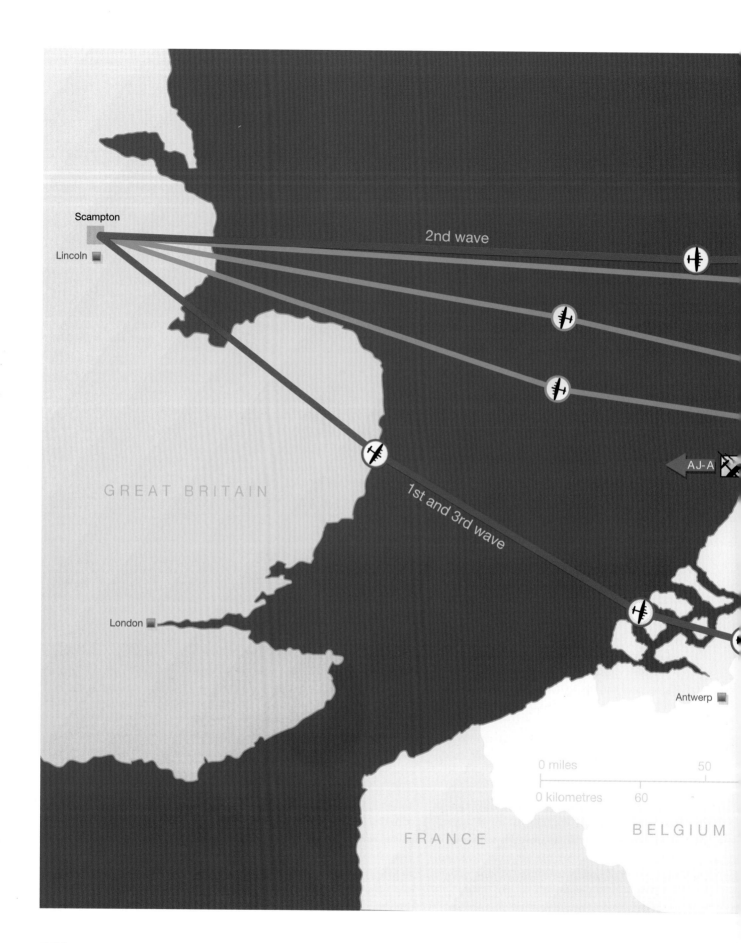

Scampton

Lincoln

2nd wave

GREAT BRITAIN

1st and 3rd wave

AJ-A

London

Antwerp

0 miles   50

0 kilometres   60

FRANCE

BELGIUM

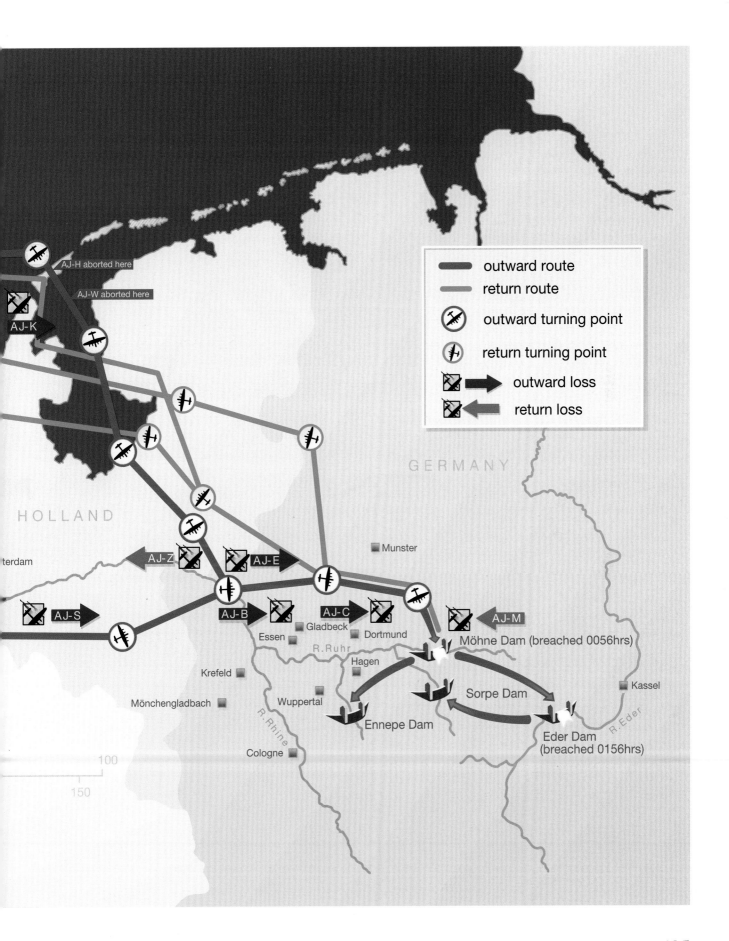

AJ-H aborted here

AJ-W aborted here

AJ-K

outward route

return route

outward turning point

return turning point

outward loss

return loss

GERMANY

HOLLAND

terdam

Munster

AJ-Z

AJ-E

AJ-S

AJ-B

AJ-C

AJ-M

Essen

Gladbeck

Dortmund

Möhne Dam (breached 0056hrs)

R.Ruhr

Hagen

Krefeld

Kassel

Sorpe Dam

Mönchengladbach

Wuppertal

R.Rhine

R.Eder

Ennepe Dam

100

Cologne

Eder Dam
(breached 0156hrs)

150

CHAPTER 5

Breaching the Dams

The moment of truth had arrived. It marked the culmination of months of intensive training by Gibson and his crews, not to mention years of toil and trial by Barnes Wallis, who had invented the bouncing bomb. As Gibson began his attack he called up Hopgood, his deputy in AJ-M: 'Hello, "M for Mother". Stand by to take over if anything happens.'

Skimming over the tree-tops of the Hever promontory, Plt Off Torger Taerum, the navigator, switched on the twin Aldis lamps and talked Gibson down to the attack height as he banked AJ-G onto the final leg towards the

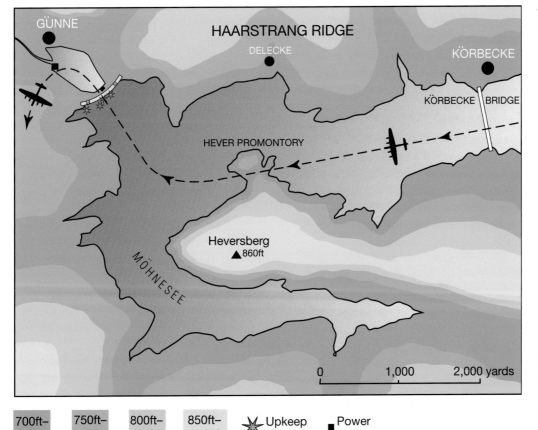

GÜNNE

HAARSTRANG RIDGE

DELECKE

KÖRBECKE

KÖRBECKE BRIDGE

HEVER PROMONTORY

Heversberg
▲860ft

MÖHNESEE

0   1,000   2,000 yards

| 700ft–750ft | 750ft–800ft | 800ft–850ft | 850ft–1,000ft | ✴ Upkeep exploded | ■ Power Station |

target. The Lancaster was now established at a height of 60ft and a speed of 230mph, but Gibson sweated at the controls of the heavy bomber to keep her dead on track towards the great dam wall that loomed menacingly ahead in the clear light of the moon.

A ferocious curtain of twinkling flak was hurled towards them. Appearing lazy at first, its glowing tracers seemed to suddenly accelerate as they hissed past.

Flt Lt Bob Hutchison, the wireless operator, checked the rotation speed of the Upkeep mine at 500rpm, while down in the bomb aimer's compartment in the nose, Plt Off Fred Spafford watched the glistening black waters of the lake rush by beneath him as he lined up the twin towers in his Dann sight.

Immediately above Spafford in the front turret, Flt Sgt George Deering opened up with everything he had, hosing the towers of the dam with tracer from his twin .303in Brownings. Gibson's description of the final moments leading to his attack are memorable:

'Spam said "Left – little more left – steady – steady – steady – coming up." Of the next few seconds I remember only a series of kaleidoscopic incidents. The chatter from Joe's front guns pushing out tracers which bounced off the left-hand flak tower. Pulford crouching beside me. The smell of burnt cordite. The cold sweat underneath my oxygen mask. The tracers flashing past the windows – they all seemed the same colour now – and the inaccuracy of the gun positions near the power station; they were firing in the wrong direction. The closeness of the dam wall. Spam's exultant, "Mine gone." Hutch's red Very lights to blind the flak gunners. The speed of the whole thing.'

AJ-G thundered over the dam wall and from his vantage point in the rear turret, Flt Lt Dick Trevor-Roper could see their weapon bouncing across the lake to hit the dam. As they circled round in the moonlit sky, Gibson's crew witnessed the terrific explosion as their mine detonated, throwing a huge column of seething white water hundreds of feet into the air. They seemed certain that with such a blast the dam could not possibly hold. 'The surface of the lake and the water had become broken and

furious,' recalled Gibson, 'as though it were being lashed by a gale. At first we thought that the dam itself had broken because great sheets of water were slopping over the top of the wall like a gigantic basin.' But once the waters of the lake had subsided it became evident that the dam had held. Hutchison signalled 5 Group HQ 'Goner 68A', which indicated that their mine had exploded but without breaching the dam.

Gibson called up Hopgood to attack, and M for Mother began its run-in over the trees of the Hever promontory towards the dam. The twin Aldis spotlights could be clearly seen by Gibson's crew as Hopgood's Lancaster descended over the lake to the bombing height of 60ft. But the enemy flak gunners had now got an idea from which direction the attack was coming and they opened up with everything they had, pouring deadly ribbons of tracer into M for Mother. When still about 300ft away from the dam wall Hopgood's Lancaster was hit in two engines and set on fire, and soon a tongue of vivid orange flame trailed from a ruptured fuel tank. In all the pandemonium Hopgood's bomb aimer, Plt Off Jim Fraser, released his Upkeep mine too late and instead of hitting the wall of the dam it bounced over the parapet, landing on the power station below that housed seven electrical transformers. There it exploded with a blinding flash. M for Mother staggered on for a short distance, Hopgood wrestling with the controls, desperately trying to gain height so that his crew could bale out, but the Lancaster was seen to explode in mid-air. One wing fell off and the wreckage tumbled into a meadow near the village of Ostonnen some three miles beyond the dam, where it burnt fiercely. Miraculously, Plt Offs Jim Fraser and Tony Burcher baled out and survived to become prisoners of war, but Sgt John Minchin was unlucky when his parachute failed to open fully and he fell to his death.

Gibson called Martin into the attack at 00.38hrs. To draw some of the enemy fire off P for Popsy, Gibson flew slightly ahead of Martin before turning G for George over the dam to engage flak positions beyond the wall. Despite his aircraft receiving some hits, bomb aimer Flt Lt Bob Hay released his Upkeep weapon. Moments later a huge explosion shook the waters of the lake once again and a plume of white spray was hurled hundreds of feet skywards. And once more, when the waters had subsided, the dam had still not been breached. Flg Off Chambers transmitted 'Goner 58A' to 5 Group HQ, informing them of another failure.

Next in line for the attack was Dinghy Young in AJ-A, who was accompanied on his run-in to the target by Martin in AJ-P, in a further attempt to draw some of the enemy flak. Gibson flew beyond the dam wall for his gunners to engage the enemy flak positions from the other side, switching on his aircraft identification lights to distract them from the approach of Young's Lancaster. AJ-A's Upkeep was released and hit the dam wall as intended. A huge explosion ensued, followed by a towering column of white water – but the dam held. 'Goner 78A' was transmitted to 5 Group HQ telling them of a further failure.

When at last the water had subsided, Gibson called up number five, David Maltby in AJ-J. This time, Gibson and Martin engaged enemy flak positions from the lake side of the dam as Maltby made his approach. From the cockpit of J for Jig he could make out that the dam structure had indeed been damaged by Young's Upkeep and that the crown of the wall was already crumbling. At 00.49hrs Maltby released his mine, which bounced four times across the glassy black water before it struck the dam wall and exploded, throwing a glistening white water spout 1,000ft into the night sky. For some unexplained reason, Maltby's wireless operator, Sgt Stone, sent another 'Goner 78A' message to HQ at Grantham before waiting to observe the result of their attack. Gibson, realising that time was getting short, called up Dave Shannon in AJ-L and told him to prepare to attack. As he turned in to make his bombing run, Gibson noticed to his amazement that water was beginning to pour through the shattered dam wall.

'I heard someone shout, "I think she has gone! I think she has gone!" Other voices took up the cry and quickly I said, "Stand by until I make a recco."' Gibson ordered

Shannon to abort his attack and turn away from the target, before flying towards the dam himself to take a closer look. 'Now there was no doubt about it; there was a great breach 100yds across, and the water, looking like stirred porridge in the moonlight, was gushing out and rolling into the Ruhr Valley. . . .'

At 00.56hrs, Gibson ordered Hutchison to tap out the signal 'Nigger' (the code word for success) to Grantham, who in turn repeated the message back to Hutchison for confirmation. The seven Lancasters that had survived so far came down from the hills around the lake, where they had been standing off, to have a closer look and see what had been done. Most of the flak had stopped by now, except for a lone gunner on the dam itself, but he was quickly silenced by a well-aimed burst of .303 from one of the Lancasters' gunners.

Writing in *Enemy Coast Ahead*, Gibson recalls: 'Now it was all quiet, except for the roar of the water which steamed and hissed its way from its 150-foot head. Then we began to shout and scream like madmen over the R/T, for this was a tremendous sight, a sight which probably no man will ever see again.'

Conscious of the fact that they had other dams to attack, Gibson silenced the R/T chatter and then called up all aircraft, telling Martin and Maltby to head for home and the rest (Shannon, Maudslay and Knight, with Young as deputy leader) to follow him to the Eder dam, 50 miles and 14 minutes' flying time to the south-east of the Möhne. They set course from the southern tip of the Möhne lake, which was already fast emptying itself of 176 million cubic yards of water. After some tricky low flying along the winding valleys that led to the Eder lake, the five aircraft finally reached their second target. It was not easy to pinpoint the dam itself because fog was already forming in the valleys, making it difficult to distinguish one part of the reservoir filled with water from another valley filled with fog.

Circling to allow Maudslay, Shannon and Astell to catch up, Gibson called up on the R/T to ask if they could see the target. Dave

OVERLEAF *Gibson and Martin use their Lancasters to draw enemy fire away from 'Dinghy' Young in AJ-A as he releases his Upkeep weapon over the Möhne lake. It took five Upkeeps to breach the wall of the Möhne, with Maltby's weapon finally cracking open the structure at 00.56hrs. (From an original painting by Nicolas Trudgian, courtesy of The Military Gallery, Bath)*

Shannon answered faintly that he thought he was nearby but couldn't find the dam. To aid him in identifying the Eder, Gibson fired a red Very light over the top of the dam, and within a few minutes all five Lancasters had rendezvoused and were flying a left-hand orbit over the target.

Situated in a deep valley surrounded by high hills densely clad with pine forest, the Eder dam was much more inaccessible and altogether a more difficult target than the Möhne. North of the dam lay the impressive medieval Waldeck castle with its commanding views across the Eder lake. To make a successful approach to the dam itself, the Lancasters would need to dive steeply over the castle from 1,000ft, then fly along the shallow gorge that led onto the lake, before encountering the wooded Hammerberg spit which formed a natural barrier in front of the dam itself. A tight turn to port would then be made over the spit, followed by a drop down to the attack height of 60ft for the run-in to the target, now less than a mile distant. If the flying

was demanding, there was one consolation in that the dam had no flak defences.

Conscious of time ticking away and dawn drawing ever nearer, Gibson ordered Shannon to commence his attack. He circled wide and then turned L for Love to go in. Diving down rather too steeply, sparks came from his engines as he had to pull out at full boost to avoid hitting the hillside. He tried three or more times without releasing his mine, unable to establish himself at the correct height for the attack after executing the steep dive followed by the sharp turn over the Hammerberg spit. He stepped aside to allow Maudslay to commence his attack, but he too found it difficult to achieve the correct height and speed in two abortive attempts. Shannon returned to the fray and made two dummy runs before finally releasing his mine at 01.39hrs. The weapon was seen to strike the dam wall and explode, followed by a towering column of white water that reached almost 1,000ft into the sky. Maudslay then began his third run up to the dam and dropped his mine, but it was

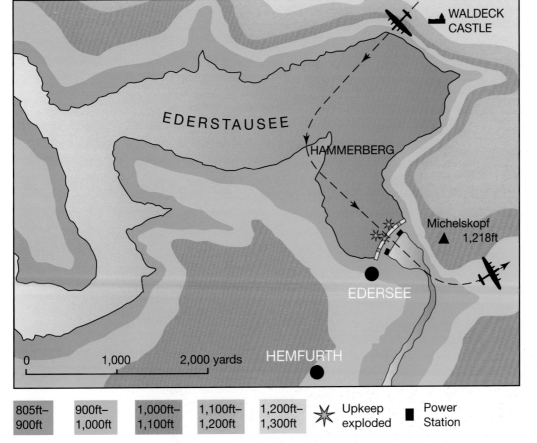

released too late. The weapon struck the dam parapet and exploded on contact with a 'slow, yellow, vivid flame which lit up the whole valley like daylight for just a few seconds'. Maudslay had flown on over the dam and appeared to be in trouble now as his Lancaster was seen banking steeply before disappearing from view. At the time it was assumed that he had crashed after being caught in the blast from his Upkeep mine, but it was later discovered that he had crossed the dam before the mine had exploded and was on his way home when he fell victim to flak at Emmerich/Klein-Netterden at 02.36hrs.

The Eder dam was still unbroken so Gibson called up Astell at 01.47hrs, but received no reply. Unknown to Gibson, Astell and his crew were dead, their Lancaster having crashed just inside the German border 97 minutes earlier. Now, only Knight in AJ-N was available to breach the Eder, and Gibson ordered him in to attack. With the last Upkeep left to do the job, he too encountered the same difficulties that Shannon and Maudslay had done earlier, but on his second run Mother Luck was on his side. Gibson recalls how 'we were flying above him, and about 400 yards to the right,

and saw his mine hit the water. We saw where it sank. We saw the tremendous earthquake which shook the base of the dam, and then, as if a gigantic hand had punched a hole through cardboard, the whole thing collapsed.' Knight and his engineer, Sgt Ray Grayston, required all their strength to haul AJ-N up and out from behind the dam to clear the high ground of the Michelskopf that loomed ahead.

At 01.54hrs, Hutchison sent the triumphant signal 'Dinghy' to 5 Group HQ, telling them the good news of the demise of the Eder dam. By now, Shannon and Knight had already turned for home and they set course for the Möhne lake to see for themselves how it had been emptying. Base signalled Hutchison, asking if they had any more aircraft in their wave available to attack the third target. The answer was 'No, none.'

At the Sorpe dam, 6 miles south-west of the Möhne, Joe McCarthy (of the second wave) and Ken Brown (third wave) had already completed their attacks, after making twelve dummy runs each before dropping their mines. The second wave of Lancasters had taken off before Gibson and had flown the northerly route across the North Sea to the Sorpe.

OPPOSITE *A pilot's-eye view from Waldeck castle, looking down onto the Ederstausee, with the Hammerberg spit in the middle foreground, and beyond (half-hidden by the forested promontory on the left) is the Eder dam itself. Behind the dam is the Michelskopf, the high ground that the attacking aircraft needed to climb and bank hard to avoid after releasing their mines. From this photograph, it can be appreciated how the topography around the Eder lake made it extremely difficult to fly an accurate approach to the dam.* (Richard Simms)

LEFT *Further reconnaissance photographs painted a similar picture of destruction at the Eder dam, where it took three Upkeeps to break open the dam wall.* (IWM CH9750)

To confuse the enemy defences and keep them guessing as to the real intentions of the bombers, they made their landfall some 125 miles to the north, but over the Dutch island of Texel the second wave suffered its first casualty. Light flak was responsible for damage inflicted on Flt Lt Les Munro's Lancaster (AJ-W), which lost both its VHF radio and its intercom as a result, forcing him to abort his sortie and return to Scampton, where he landed at 00.30hrs, the Upkeep still clasped beneath the belly of W for William.

Crossing the Dutch coast, Plt Off Vernon Byers in AJ-K was shot down by a 105mm flak gun, his aircraft crashing into the sea

RIGHT *The Sorpe defied the combined efforts of Flt Lt Joe McCarthy (AJ-T) and Sgt Ken Brown (AJ-F) to make a breach in its concrete and earth wall. Two mines were dropped and the parapet damaged for a length of about 200ft, but the dam remained largely unscathed.* (Crown Copyright)

in flames off the southern tip of Texel. Meanwhile, Flg Off Geoff Rice in Lancaster AJ-H was flying so low that his aircraft grazed the surface of the sea near the island of Vlieland, the impact ripping off the Upkeep mine and tearing a gaping hole in the Lancaster's belly. With the fuselage

BELOW *Map of the Sorpe dam and its environs, showing the local topography and the direction of attack.* (Bow Watkinson)

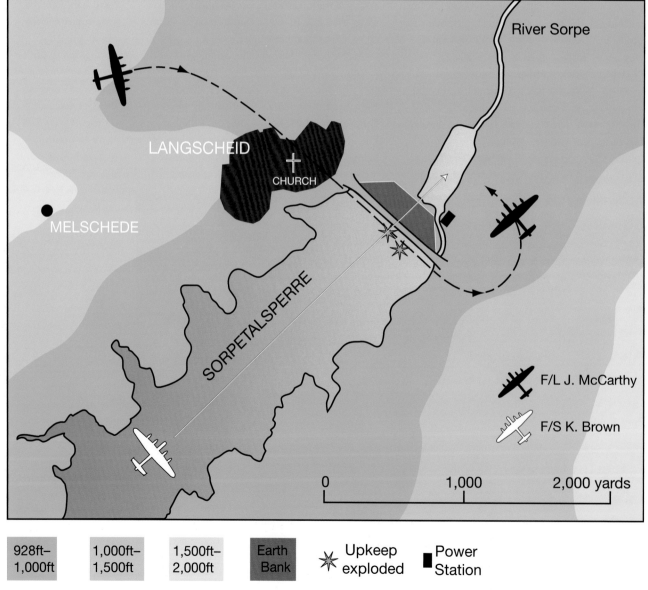

SORPE DAM
(After attack)
K 1559
Neg. No. 24689

RIGHT *Just how thoroughly the mine was examined can be appreciated from these scale drawings of the 'British Spinning Water Bomb' produced by the Germans.*

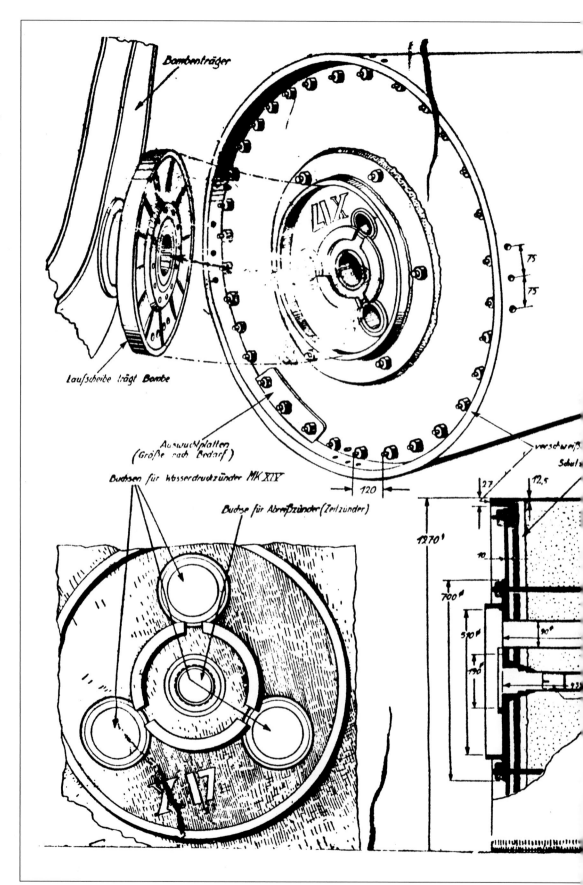

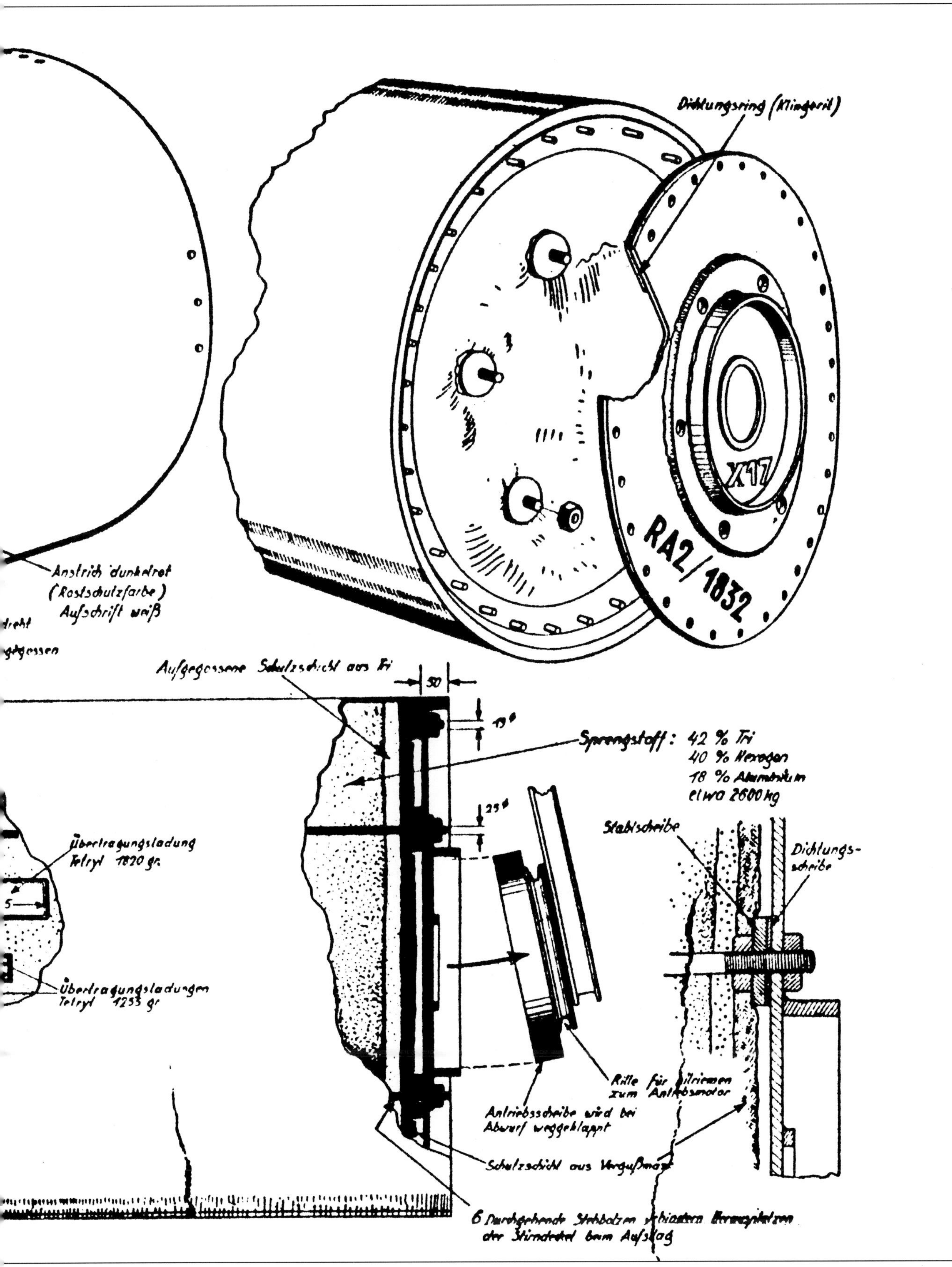

Dichtungsring (Klingerit)

RA2/1832

X17

Anstrich dunkelrot
(Rostschutzfarbe)
Aufschrift weiß

dreht

ghgossen

Aufgegossene Schutzschicht aus Tri

50

Sprengstoff: 42 % Tri
40 % Hexogen
18 % Aluminium
etwa 2600 kg

Übertragungsladung
Tetryl 1820 gr.

Übertragungsladungen
Tetryl 1255 gr

Stahlscheibe

Dichtungs-
scheibe

Rille für Riemen
zum Antriebsmotor

Antriebsscheibe wird bei
Abwurf weggeklappt

Schutzschicht aus Vergußmasse

6 Durchgehende Stahbolzen verhindern Herauszielzen
der Stirnwand beim Aufslag

ABOVE *When Flt Lt Bob Barlow's Lancaster (AJ-E) collided with an electricity pylon and crashed at Haldern-Herken, its Upkeep rolled clear of the wreckage and miraculously failed to go off. The mine was later recovered and defused by German bomb disposal experts, who succeeded in discovering many of its secrets.* **(via Alfred Price)**

awash with sea water, he was forced to abort the sortie and nurse his badly damaged aircraft back to Scampton, where he landed at 00.50hrs, lucky to have made it home.

The perilous nature of low flying in a heavy bomber aircraft at night claimed the lives of Flt Lt Bob Barlow and his crew in Lancaster AJ-E. They struck the top of an electricity pylon along the River Rhine near Rees and the aircraft crashed in flames at Haldern-Herken. Their Upkeep did not explode on impact and the self-destruction charge failed to go off. The mine was successfully defused by a German bomb disposal team and eventually contributed a great deal to the Nazis' knowledge of the bouncing bomb.

Having taken off 34 minutes late due to a string of technical problems, McCarthy flew at 200mph, and had made up some of the lost time when he crossed the Dutch coast at Vlieland at 23.31hrs. By now the German flak gunners were wide awake and looking for trouble, but flying at tree-top height McCarthy skilfully avoided major incident, although AJ-T collected a bullet in the starboard undercarriage nacelle. Four of the five aircraft in the second wave had either been forced to abort or had crashed, leaving only McCarthy to continue to the Sorpe, where he arrived at about 00.15hrs. He encountered the same problem that Gibson and the others had found at the Eder, with thick mist in the valleys causing difficulty in pinpointing the dam. When at last the dam was identified it was lit by bright moonlight from a cloudless sky, and McCarthy began his bombing run that led him over the sleeping village of Langscheid and along the crest of the 2,297ft-long dam wall. The reserve aircraft in which he was flying had not been fitted with the twin Aldis spotlights that were necessary for accurate height keeping, and so it took nine attempts before McCarthy's bomb aimer, Sgt George Johnson, was satisfied with AJ-T's height and line of flight. At 00.46hrs, on the tenth run, Johnson released his Upkeep mine close to the centre of the dam wall, without any rotation and from a height of about 30ft. The resulting explosion sent a huge shower of water high into the sky, but when McCarthy flew back across the dam to inspect the result of his attack it became clear that the dam wall itself had survived, with only the parapet suffering damage.

Turning his Lancaster about and setting a course for home, McCarthy soon overflew what was left of the Möhne dam and its fast-emptying lake, but before long AJ-T became lost. In time the crew found themselves flying over the heavily defended railway marshalling yards at Hamm, at the perilously low height of 50ft – and certainly not the place for a heavy bomber to linger. Fortunately luck was on their side and they managed to escape without damage by heading towards the cluster of lakes near Dulmen. Still uncertain of their position, McCarthy finally opted to retrace the track of their outward-bound route instead of following the official track agreed at the briefing. AJ-T landed back on Scampton's turf at 03.23hrs, but the flak hit they had taken on the outward flight had punctured a main wheel tyre, and so the touchdown was a little bumpy.

Flt Sgt Ken Brown had taken off at 00.12hrs, the third aircraft in the reserve wave, and crossed the enemy coast at 01.30hrs. Flying at low level over the hostile landscape of occupied Europe, AJ-F received the unwelcome attention of light flak. On several occasions Brown was forced to take violent evasive action when electricity pylons and tall trees loomed out of the darkness ahead of his aircraft. Nearing the target area,

AJ-F's wireless operator received word from 5 Group HQ that the Möhne dam had been breached and ordering them to the Sorpe. Poor visibility owing to fog in the valleys caused problems in identifying the dam, but as luck would have it the visibility improved in its immediate vicinity and Brown was able to carry out his first attack run. But, as with McCarthy before him, the Sorpe proved a difficult nut to crack and it took nine attempts before Brown's Upkeep mine was finally dropped at 03.14hrs. Unlike McCarthy, Brown took a head-on approach to the dam across the lake and dropped his mine against the wall, but again without any spin on the weapon. In due course, the tower of water that followed the explosion fell away to reveal to eager eyes in the circling Lancaster that the dam wall was still intact. However, further damage had been done to the parapet of the dam and its stone crest had begun to crumble. The signal, 'Goner 78C', was transmitted to Grantham by Brown's wireless operator at 03.23hrs: their mine had exploded against the dam wall but had not breached it.

Brown and his crew beat a path for home. Flying over the spectacular silver ribbon of floods that by now had engulfed the hapless valley below the Möhne dam, they flew on, falling foul of accurate predicted flak and blinding searchlights at Hamm, and later when crossing the Zuider Zee. At such low level, the glare of the searchlights that suffused the cockpit of AJ-F could have blinded Brown, but he crouched as low in the cockpit as he dared while still flying the aircraft. By dint of some masterly low flying and a strong helping of good luck, AJ-F escaped disaster to cross the North Sea in the early morning light and land safely at Scampton at 05.33hrs.

Having fallen behind schedule since becoming the last Lancaster to take off, AJ-Y captained by Flt Sgt Cyril Anderson became lost. En route he had been ordered to attack the Diemel dam, but at 02.28hrs his target was changed to the Sorpe. With his rear turret unserviceable and the dawn creeping ever closer, he decided to turn back. He arrived home at Scampton at 05.30hrs with his mine still on board.

The last aircraft to attempt an attack on a Ruhr dam during Operation Chastise was AJ-O captained by Plt Off Bill Townsend. Having taken off from Scampton at 00.14hrs, AJ-O made landfall over the enemy coast at 01.31hrs and suffered the unwelcome attentions of light flak along much of its flight path as it thundered across Germany at tree-top height. At 02.22hrs, Grantham signalled AJ-O to attack the Ennepe dam, the Möhne and Eder having been breached by this point. Routeing via the Möhne dam, it was with some difficulty that Townsend eventually found the Ennepe, thanks to rising mist in the surrounding valleys. Circling over the lake, it quickly became apparent to him and his bomb aimer, Sgt C.E. Franklin, that the approach to the dam was going to be very difficult due to a number of topographical factors. In the end it took them until their fourth attempt before Franklin was happy with the height, speed and line of their approach, to release his mine at 03.37hrs. Climbing up and over the tree-clad hills behind the dam, Townsend banked AJ-O around and turned back for a low pass over the dam to inspect the damage made by his mine. The characteristic explosion of their mine had been followed by a towering

LEFT *Lying broken on a beach in Holland, the wreckage of a Lancaster bears silent witness to the losses sustained by 617 Squadron on the dams raid. This aircraft is possibly ED877/ AJ-A, flown by Sqn Ldr Henry 'Dinghy' Young, shot down crossing the Dutch coast north of IJmuiden on its homeward journey from bombing the Möhne dam. (Crown Copyright)*

waterspout, but the weapon had sunk far short of the wall and failed to breach the dam. At 04.11hrs AJ-O's wireless operator, Flt Sgt George Chalmers, sent 'Goner 58E' to HQ at Grantham.

Like Brown, Townsend flew back over the fast-emptying Möhne dam before setting a course for home, a journey that was anything but an enjoyable experience. Pushing the control column forward and taking AJ-O down among the weeds to fly her as fast as he dared, Townsend needed his full concentration to avoid high-tension cables and towering trees that loomed ahead in their path. They crossed over the enemy coast after attracting the unwelcome attention of enemy flak and searchlights and made it safely back to Scampton, where AJ-O landed at 06.15hrs, the final aircraft to arrive home from Operation Chastise.

A little over one hour after Townsend had throttled back AJ-O's over-stressed Merlins, switched off and climbed exhausted from the aircraft with his crew onto Scampton's sweet-smelling grass, a solitary PR Spitfire took off from RAF Benson and headed into the morning sun for the Ruhr dams more than 300 miles distant.

OVERLEAF
Homeward bound: after bombing the Eder dam, Flt Lt David Shannon in Lancaster AJ-L races the dawn for home, at low level across the flat landscape of Holland. (From an original painting by Nicolas Trudgian, courtesy of The Military Gallery, Bath)

CHAPTER 6

The Aftermath

Germany

In the Ruhr and Eder valleys a disaster of biblical proportions had been unleashed. The force of the floodwaters as they bore down the valleys from the breaches in the Möhne and Eder dams was so great that the waters swept away almost everything in their deafening path. People's homes were dashed to pieces

OPPOSITE *The sheer scale of the catastrophe at the Möhne dam can be appreciated from this dramatic photograph. In the foreground lies a tangle of anti-torpedo netting and floats, washed through the breach by the relentless floodwaters.* (Bundesarchiv 101I/637/4192/27)

BELOW *Torrents of water were still rushing through the breach in the Möhne dam twelve hours after the raid.* (IWM HU4594)

like so much matchwood, railway bridges torn down, trees uprooted, people and livestock carried away in the unrelenting torrent. Some observers reported seeing trees stripped of their bark, with railway lines wrapped around them like giant corkscrews.

Back in England, 542 Squadron had been warned of the time of the attack and that photo-reconnaissance would be required to monitor the result. The crews were up early to study the weather conditions, which appeared to be favourable. At 07.30hrs on the morning of the 17th, a lone Spitfire PRXI piloted by Flg Off Jerry Fray took off from RAF Benson and climbed out over the North Sea, heading for Germany and the Ruhr dams. Its mission was to arrive over the target at the first photographic light and photograph the results of the raids.

Several hundred miles ahead of Fray and his Spitfire, flooding along the Ruhr Valley below the Möhne dam now extended for about 40 miles. The town of Neheim, which lay several miles downstream from the dam

itself, had been cut clean in two by the floodwaters. At the valley's narrowest point between Niederense and Neheim, the water had achieved speeds of up to 18ft/sec and it had reportedly reached a level of more than 45ft.

As luck would have it, visibility was good and this promised Fray some clear photographs to take back to Benson. At a distance of about 150 miles from the Möhne dam, Fray could see the chemical haze that hung over the German industrial heartland of the Ruhr, and, turning his head slightly, away to the east he noticed what he took to be a bank of cloud. As he flew closer it became apparent that this cloud was in fact the effect of the sun glinting on the floodwaters that had been unleashed from the dams some 30,000ft beneath him. Soon the sheer enormity of the inundation that had hit the Ruhr Valley became clear, and as he neared the Möhne dam he estimated that the floodwaters were about a mile wide. Eight hours after the attack, water was still gushing through the breach in the dam wall at a rate

In this unusual view along the parapet of the Möhne dam, pieces of masonry are scattered on the roadway in the foreground that stops abruptly with the yawning breach in the dam wall. In the background can be seen the northern shore of the lake where the massive drop in water level is immediately apparent. (Bundesarchiv 101I/637/4192/12)

of between 53,000 and 70,000 cubic ft/sec, and the level of the water in the reservoir had fallen dramatically, leaving exposed brown mud flats around the edges. The upper reaches of the lake were completely dry, except for the small portion where the sluice gates had been closed. He carried out his photographic run over the Möhne before flying on to the Eder dam.

As Fray looked down from his Spitfire cockpit onto the virtually empty reservoir 6 miles beneath him, he observed that the damage in the Eder Valley was far greater. This was due largely to the fact that the breach in the dam was wider than that at the Möhne, allowing more than three-quarters of the contents of the reservoir to escape. In reality, the lake would have been almost impossible to pinpoint had it not been for the tell-tale white stain of water still pouring from the breach in the dam wall. Two days after the attack, water was still gushing through the breach. Fray made a second run over the Eder to take further photographs, but seeing two unidentified aircraft approaching from the north-east he decided to cut short his sortie and beat it home.

Writing not long afterwards in the RAF's secret *Coastal Command Quarterly Review* (the RAF's PR squadrons were under the operational control of Coastal Command), Fray recalls his homecoming to Benson:

'While I was landing, I could see scrambled egg at the end of the runway. It was the station commander and I wondered if I had done anything wrong. But he was only waiting to welcome me home. When I landed he came up to me and said, "Have they hit them?" and I was able to answer, "Yes, they've pranged two of them properly. The floods are spreading for miles." So he went off to telephone the news to Bomber Command.'

At Benson the atmosphere was electric as the films were rushed from Fray's Spitfire and immediately developed. The first negatives to be processed from the damage assessment sortie were taken out of the drying cabinet and placed on the light table for examination. Everyone was there, from the station commander down, and they all crowded around Flt Lt Ronald Gillanders, who was in charge of the day shift of damage interpreters at Medmenham. He had been ordered over to Benson by the Air Ministry so as to be there when Fray landed. As soon as the negatives were ready for viewing, he was to telephone Gp Capt McNeil, Assistant Director of Photographic Intelligence at the Air Ministry, with the results of the initial interpretation.

The first frames of negatives showed nothing but floodwater – acres of it. Then Gillanders came to the Möhne dam and with the pin-sharp negative before him, he phoned McNeil – there was a gap right in the centre of the dam, about 200ft across, and water was pouring through it.

Speaking afterwards, Gillanders admitted to being a little worried:

'For a minute I did not recognise the place. I feared for a moment that they had bombed the wrong dam. I looked for the power station, but it had gone. The place which I had studied in great detail for many months looked completely different, and it was only on a second look that I recognised the familiar landmarks and realised that the reservoir was practically empty.'

Once all the photographs had been printed and interpreted it became very clear that the Möhne and Eder dams had been breached, but that the Sorpe was damaged and still intact. Benson despatched a further PR sortie at 10.45hrs and a third one in the same afternoon to add to the first coverage obtained by Fray.

ABOVE *A further view of the massive 230ft-breach in the wall of the Eder dam, probably photographed in the late afternoon of 17 May. Water pours through the breach at the rate of some 1.8 million gallons per second.* (RAF Museum PC71/19/795)

OVERLEAF

A photographic mosaic of the Möhne lake and its hinterland. The sheer size of the lake can be appreciated when compared to the dam itself, seen at top left. (Bruce Robertson collection)

ABOVE *One of the massive water pipes used to feed the turbines of the main power station that once stood in the shadow of the Möhne dam. The building was destroyed by Hopgood's Upkeep weapon and then washed away by the raging floodwaters when the dam was finally breached.* (Bundesarchiv 1011/637/4192/30)

RIGHT *Debris litters the floor of the compensating basin in the shadow of the Möhne dam.* (Bundesarchiv 1011/637/4192/23)

Photo-reconnaissance confirmed that material damage in both the Ruhr and Eder valleys was extensive, but was far more serious along the Möhne and Ruhr valleys, where the river beds were badly silted up below Neheim. In places the rivers had altered their course and in time it would be necessary to divert them back along their old beds. Large gravel banks had also formed and effectively cut off the valley, hindering drainage of the floodwaters. In the shadow of the Möhne dam wall, the power station had been completely destroyed, along with the compensating basin, while the smaller power station situated a little further south was so heavily damaged as to be beyond repair. Further downstream, heavy damage had been caused to many more waterworks and power stations, mainly through the action of mud, silt and the undermining of the structures.

Writing after the war in his memoirs, *Inside the Third Reich*, Hitler's Armaments Minister Albert Speer recalled:

'The report that reached me in the early hours of the morning was most alarming. The largest of the dams, the Möhne dam, had been shattered and the reservoir emptied. As yet there were no reports on the three other dams. At dawn we landed at Werl airfield, having first surveyed the scene of devastation from above. The power plant at the foot of the shattered

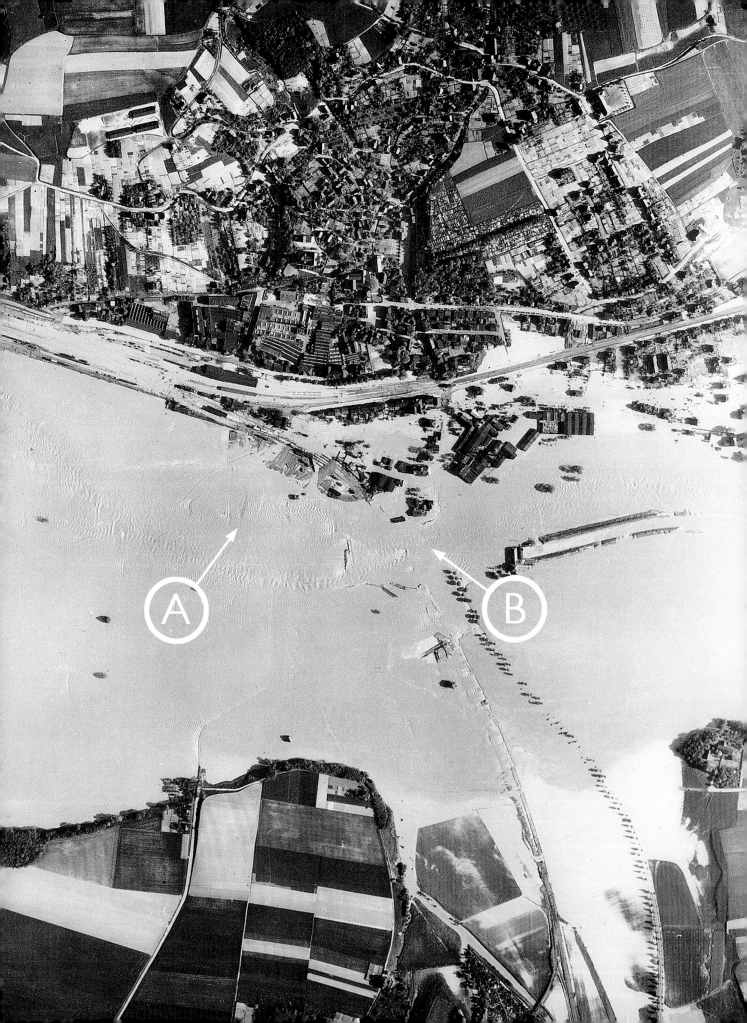

dam looked as if it had been erased, along with its turbines.'

In the Ruhr Valley, the weirs and mechanical plant at Echthausen and Wickede power stations had been totally destroyed. The weirs at Soest waterworks, Vereinigte Stahlwerke (steel works), and the power station at Frondenberg had been wrecked, and large portions of the neighbouring canal bank had caved in. More than five miles of overhead electric cables were also brought down in the area of Neheim and Frondenberg. Further afield, the waterworks dam at Gelsenkirchen had been completely destroyed, and at Dortmund the waterworks and power station were badly damaged, causing huge disruption to heavy industry and domestic supplies in the area.

Thanks to the floodwaters, the transport network and its infrastructure along the Möhne and Ruhr valleys also suffered badly. The main railway line from Hagen to Kassel was seriously damaged between Neheim and Wickede, and in places the track bed was completely washed away. At Wickede the track itself had been lifted bodily off the embankment and washed onto the lower-lying fields below. It took until 11 June for express train services to be resumed. All road and narrow-gauge railway bridges in the Möhne Valley were destroyed by the power of the floodwaters, and damage to roads was severe, ranging from potholes to the complete destruction of the roadbed and metalling.

Industry in the Möhne and Ruhr valleys was hard hit by the attack. Numerous firms lost buildings, machinery and materials, swept away by the floodwaters or seriously damaged by mud, and they were also affected by damage to electricity and water supplies. The worst-hit area was the lower Möhne Valley around Neheim: the steel works at Hagen-Kabel and Harkort-Eicken in Wetter were extensively damaged by the effects of the attack.

Albert Speer recalled that his report on the situation, which he delivered to Hitler's headquarters soon after visiting the Ruhr Valley, 'made a deep impression on the Führer'.

OPPOSITE *The Ruhr Valley at Frondenberg, 13 miles downstream from the Möhne dam. It was at this point that the floodwaters spread out across the full width of the valley. At 'A' stood a hutted camp for Russian PoWs, washed away by the inundation; at 'B' the road and rail bridges that linked Frondenberg to Menden were also swept away (and see overleaf).* (Crown Copyright)

BELOW *The floods swept away factory buildings in Neheim – the foundations in the foreground are all that remain.* (RAF Museum PC71/19/356/43)

All that remained of the double-track steel railway bridge at Frondenberg that was ripped from its piers and carried more than 330ft downstream by the floodwaters. The toppled steelwork of the bridge can be seen in the top left of the photograph, with the masonry piers towards the centre.
(Bundesarchiv 101I/637/4194/5A)

ABOVE *Flooding in the Eder Valley which resulted from the breach of the dam, and in particular the inundation of the Luftwaffe airfield at Fritzlar (seen here at centre), 15 miles south-south-west of Kassel. Hangars were flooded and the airfield was rendered completely unusable.* (IWM C5682)

Downstream from the Eder dam, the villages of Hemfurth, Affoldern, Mehlen, Bergheim and Giflitz were badly affected by the floodwaters, while several miles further on the Luftwaffe airfield at Fritzlar was completely flooded. Twenty-five road and rail bridges had been swept away, including the railway station at Giflitz and the bridge carrying the main line to Frankfurt. Serious inundations affected Hemfurth and Affoldern, as well as parts of the city of Kassel. In fact the effects of the flooding were felt in the Fulda and Weser rivers for a distance of about 300 miles from the Eder. At Hameln, more than 130 miles away, the River

Weser rose by more than 20ft in the immediate aftermath of the raid.

As for the Sorpe dam, it withstood serious damage. 'They did achieve a direct hit on the centre of the dam,' wrote Speer. 'I inspected it that same day. Fortunately the bomb hole was slightly higher than the water level. Just a few inches lower – and a small brook would have been transformed into a raging river which would have swept away the stone and earthen dam.'

Initial claims of widespread loss of life among the population of the Ruhr Valley talked of between 3,000 and 4,000 dead, but this

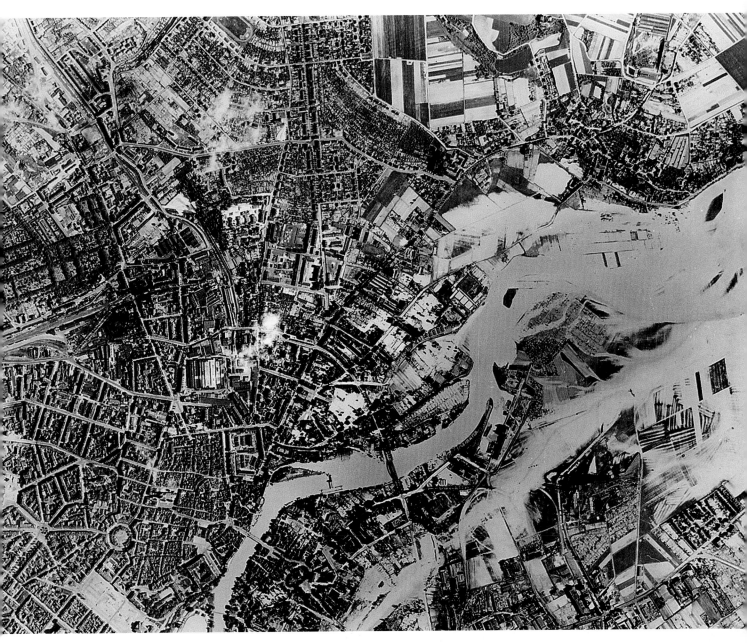

figure was soon refuted and the final death toll was eventually adjusted to 1,294, although some German sources believe it to be in excess of 1,400. Some 493 were Ukrainian women – forced labourers – although Dutch, French and Belgian prisoners of war were also among the casualties. Three months later, as the clearing up operation continued, bodies were still being found at Neheim.

By noon on the 17th the floodwaters in the Ruhr Valley had abated in Neheim and Wickede, but the valley itself had been shorn of all its familiar features by the scouring effect of the fast-moving floodwaters. In their place

had been left mounds of twisted debris, heaps of mud, metal girders, uprooted trees, furniture and personal belongings. Surprisingly, it was only a few days before water supplies had been fully restored in Neheim and its environs.

Shortly before the raid, water production in the Ruhr stood at one million cubic metres. Although this figure plummeted by three-quarters in its aftermath, within six weeks the original output had been restored. Water supplies to the city of Dortmund fell to one-fifth in a matter of hours after the raid: within three days they were back up to four-fifths.

Electricity supplies were also only

ABOVE *By 10.00am on 17 May, the floodwaters of the Eder lake had reached the town of Kassel, 37 miles downstream, where the River Fulda rose to more than 13ft above its usual level.* (Crown Copyright)

The Sorpe dam was a difficult nut to crack, mainly due to its concrete and earth core construction, and in the end it defied the RAF's attempts to breach it. However, the two Upkeep mines that were dropped succeeded in damaging the parapet structure (seen towards the centre of the wall). This led to a certain amount of water spillage from the reservoir into the compensating basin below the wall, which can be discerned from the stirred up sediment. (IWM C5897)

RIGHT *Some 18ft up from the ground, bark was stripped from tree trunks by the ferocity of the floodwaters.* (RAF Museum PC71/19/356/17)

OPPOSITE *An incredible photograph taken at Neheim showing what remains of a detached house that stood in the path of the raging floodwaters from the Möhne. This house was lucky: many more were simply carried away by the floods and dashed to pieces.* (Bundesarchiv 101I/637/4193/20)

OVERLEAF *Civilians in the Ruhr Valley queue for drinking water in the aftermath of the dams raid.* (Bundesarchiv 101I/637/4193/20)

temporarily disrupted. It was not necessary to rebuild the power station at the Möhne and the giant power plant at Herdecke was only offline for a fortnight. In any case, the Germans obtained alternative electricity supplies from generating stations that used water from the Alps.

At first sight, heavy industry appeared to have been largely unaffected: steel production in the Greater Reich and the occupied territories actually exceeded that of 1942 by 2.5 million tons.

In some respects, however, the attacks did have far-reaching effects on other parts of the Ruhr Valley's industrial infrastructure. The important waterworks at Frondenberg and Echthausen were disabled in the early hours of the 17th and were not returned to full working order until August. Official German records show that only a basic level of water supply to consumers was maintained in the aftermath of the attack.

The Ruhr suffered an 8 per cent reduction in steel output in the second half of 1943,

while the whole of north-west Germany lost 1.9 million tons of crude steel production that year. Allied air raids over the region caused a significant loss in production of crude steel, with over 600,000 metric tons lost in May and June alone. This is particularly noteworthy, since only in four other months that year did lost production exceed 100,000 tons, with the highest figure reaching 137,000 tons.

The loss of vital water supplies to coke works in the Ruhr Valley also meant that supplies to principal gas consumers were slashed by more than half on 19 May.

Rebuilding of the Möhne and Eder dams proceeded quickly under the auspices of Albert Speer and the Todt Organisation, and on 25 September the yawning gap in the Möhne's wall was finally closed, while work on the Eder was completed soon afterwards. Both reservoirs were then able to hold water from the rainfall of winter 1943–4, but due to the extensive damage suffered by both dams the level of water in the reservoirs, including the Sorpe, was reduced accordingly as a

OPPOSITE *In these views of the Eder dam taken soon after the end of the war, the parapet walling has still to be replaced (above), while the repairs to the dam wall itself (below), completed in September 1943, have failed to reinstate numbers 3, 4 and 5 vents. However, final reconstruction was not completed until June 1944.* (Both pictures TRL Ltd)

BELOW *Repairs to the Möhne dam were completed on 25 September 1943, some eleven weeks after work had begun on 9 July.* (TRL Ltd)

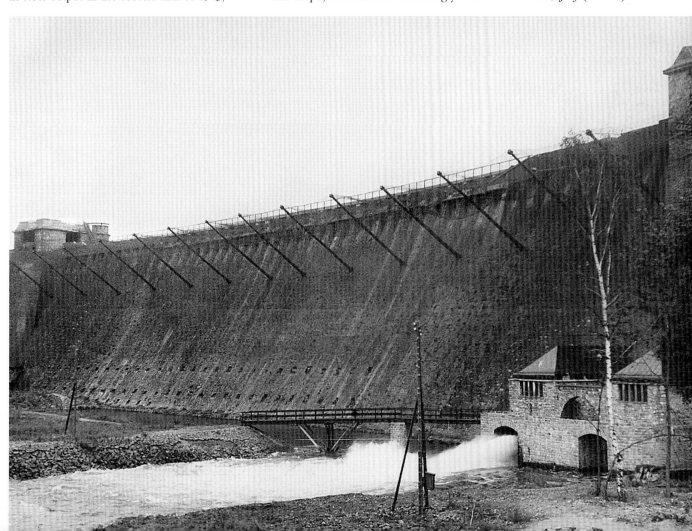

Jugendherberge Körbecke · Gruß vom schönen Möhnesee · Möhnetalsperre, Luftbild

Auf der Sperrmauer · Blick zur Sperrmauer

precaution. It was not until 1946–7, when further repairs were carried out, that they were able to operate at full capacity once more.

Nor was it only industry that suffered the consequences of the attacks. Agriculture and food supplies were hit too. The scouring effect of the floodwaters stripped away topsoil on farmland in the Möhne and Eder valleys, rendering them virtually impossible to cultivate, and they remained barren for many years to come. Loss of agricultural production in the region could not quickly be made good by supplies from elsewhere in Germany because of the widespread disruption to communications caused by Allied air raids.

The diversion of labour and resources to repair the damage caused by the raids was short-term in its effects, but the need to build and man defences at dams considered liable to future air attack represented a longer-term drain on both civilian and military resources. Some 10,000 regular troops from the Heer and Luftwaffe, plus many more from reserve units, were diverted to this task from important duties elsewhere in the Reich.

The question of how best to protect Germany's dams from future air attack occupied the minds of Nazi officialdom for many months after the raids. At the Möhne dam, the results included additional torpedo nets, special Luftwaffe fighter cover, 328ft-high aerial steel curtains stretched across the reservoir to deter low-flying aircraft, and anti-bomb and anti-rocket netting projecting out from the wall on the dam's air side. This was in addition to searchlights, barrage balloons and smokescreen equipment. Extensive provision for the defence of the Eder and Sorpe dams was also made.

But what of the civilian populations of the Ruhr and Eder valleys? The effect of the attacks on their morale is difficult to gauge. Allied bombing of the Ruhr had been going on for many years, with particular intensity between March and July 1943 in the so-called Battle of the Ruhr, during which time the RAF mounted thirty-one major raids. It is therefore difficult to separate the effects of the general bombing of the region from the specific civilian response to the dams raids. Much clearing up and

OPPOSITE TOP *Special bomb deflectors were built on the Möhne lake to prevent bombs from coming into contact with the dam wall. On the far left can be seen anti-torpedo netting.* (TRL Ltd)

OPPOSITE BOTTOM *Steel netting was erected on the valley side of the Möhne dam wall to deflect bombs. The twin towers were also reduced in height to prevent them from being used as markers again in an aerial attack.* (TRL Ltd)

ABOVE *By the 1950s the Möhne dam and lake had almost returned to normal.*

rebuilding of homes had to be undertaken in the aftermath of the floods, but civilian wrath was not simply confined to Britain and the RAF.

The competence of the Luftwaffe was called into question since defensive measures to protect the dams was so obviously lacking. Indeed, the mayor of Essen, Julius Dillgardt, who was also Chairman of the Ruhr Valley Dams Association, had been involved in protracted correspondence with the military authorities since the beginning of the war regarding the protection of the Ruhr dams from air attack. The risk of a devastating attack on the dams from the air was still considered an impossibility by the military. Only the Möhne was linked to the Luftwaffe air defence system and no smoke generators were deployed at any of the dams until after the attack. Events were to prove that it was a prime example of blinkered thinking by the Nazi military authorities, and of shutting the stable door after the horse had bolted.

Albert Speer later wrote that: 'While we were engaged in rebuilding, the British air force missed its second chance. A few bombs would have produced cave-ins at the exposed building sites, and a few fire bombs could have set the wooden scaffolding blazing.'

However, for German Intelligence, something quite unexpected came out of the raids – an intact Upkeep mine, which they were able to successfully defuse. This was the

weapon from Flt Lt Bob Barlow's Lancaster, AJ-E, which had crashed at Haldern-Herken after hitting a high-tension electricity pylon. The mine had rolled clear of the blazing wreckage, relatively undamaged, and the self-destruction charge failed to go off. It was safely defused and removed to a weapons evaluation depot at Kalkum near Düsseldorf for a thorough examination. From information obtained by the weapons experts at Kalkum and the interrogation statement of Plt Off Fraser, one of only two men to survive from Hopgood's crew, the Luftwaffe came close to uncovering the secrets of Barnes Wallis's

BELOW *A case of too little too late: barrage balloons fly over the Möhne in this German photograph taken late on 18 May.*

bouncing bomb. By September 1943, the Germans were carrying out basic tests on a design for their own bouncing bomb weapon at the Luftwaffe's Ballistics Institute and Technical Academy at Berlin-Gatow. But the critical detail they failed to discover was the depth at which the bomb was supposed to explode, and that it had to explode in contact with the dam wall.

British fears that their attacks on the German dams could be replicated by the Luftwaffe against dams in England and Wales led to enhanced defensive measures being taken at home, but the half-expected raids did not materialise. Speer himself wondered why the Luftwaffe didn't launch similar pinpoint attacks against key industrial targets in Britain. He raised this matter with Hitler at the end of May 1943, but the Führer appeared uninterested, commenting that the Luftwaffe's commanders would not be receptive to advice from Speer's industrialist advisers. In any case, he had already discussed this matter with General Oberst Jeschonnek (Göring's second in command) on several occasions, but they had failed to reach a decision. Once again, Hitler had thrown away a golden opportunity to do real damage to Britain's war economy.

BELOW *A series of enhanced defensive measures were taken in Britain to defend its dams against a similar attack from the Luftwaffe. This is Graig Goch dam in the Elan Valley near Rhayader, not far from the Nant-y-Gro dam which was used by Barnes Wallis in his early trials for Upkeep.*

RIGHT *A wintry view of the Möhne dam, pictured from the Soest side of the lake in the 1990s.* (Richard Simms)

RIGHT *In this post-war photograph of the Eder dam, the repaired section of wall can be clearly seen in the left foreground. On the horizon is Waldeck castle, which dominates the Eder reservoir.* (Richard Simms)

RIGHT *The Eder dam and lake seen in the late 1990s.* (Eder-Touristic Gmbh)

LEFT *An RAF Phantom of 17 Squadron passes over the Möhne dam in 1974.* (RAF Germany)

BELOW *A post-war aerial view of the Möhne dam from the reservoir side, looking towards the compensating basin. The main power station below the dam wall that was destroyed by Hopgood's Upkeep has never been rebuilt.* (Bruce Robertson collection)

The Daily Telegraph and Morning Post

No. 27,435 LONDON, TUESDAY, MAY 18, 1943 Printed in LONDON and MANCHESTER PRICE 1½d.

4 A.M.

R.A.F. BLOW UP THREE KEY DAMS IN GERMANY

DEVASTATION SWEEPS DOWN RUHR VALLEY

BRIDGES AND POWER PLANTS ENGULFED

ADVANCING FLOODS STILL SPREADING FAST

With one single blow the R.A.F. has precipitated what may prove to be the greatest industrial disaster yet inflicted on Germany in this war.

A force of Lancasters, loaded with mines and with crews specially trained for the task, early yesterday morning attacked and destroyed the great dams on the Mohne and Sorpe rivers, tributaries of the Ruhr, and also the dam on the Eder River.

To-day walls of water sweeping down the Ruhr and Eder valleys are carrying everything before them.

The Air Ministry announced last night that a partial reconnaissance of the Ruhr Valley and the district near the Eder dam shows that the floods are spreading fast.

"The waters are sweeping down the Ruhr Valley," it stated. "Railways and road bridges are broken down. Hydro-electrical power stations are destroyed or damaged, a railway marshalling yard is under water.

"The floods from the breached Eder dam are already as great as the floods in the Ruhr Valley, but the country here is flatter and the water likely to spread over a greater area."

GERMANS ADMIT HEAVY CASUALTIES

The German communiqué yesterday, admitting that two dams had been "damaged"—it did not specify the area—said "heavy casualties were caused among the civilian population by the resulting floods." That was as much as the people of Germany were allowed to know. There was no reference to the disaster in later news broadcasts from Berlin.

The pilots, on their return, reported seeing in the moonlight huge breaches in the dams with water bursting through. They saw a power-station below the Mohne dam swept away in the flood and a 30ft high wall of water rumbling down the Eder valley.

Reporting personally to Air Chief Marshal Sir Arthur Harris, Chief of Bomber Command, Wing Cmdr. G. P. Gibson, who led the raid, said the immediate results of the destruction of the dams were far beyond their expectations.

Wing Cmdr. Gibson was the first to attack the Mohne Dam. After dropping his load he flew up and down drawing the enemy's fire to give the following planes a better chance of success. It was not until the fourth load had been dropped that the dam was first breached.

Air reconnaissance yesterday showed that there was a 100-yard gap in it.

There was no indication last night of the number of Lancasters engaged, but, although the loss of eight machines and their crews on an attack on such an objective must be regarded as fairly heavy, the complete success of the operation tells its own story of the worth of the sacrifice.

PARALYSING INDUSTRY

Apart from the cumulative damage caused by the floods, there is a firm basis for believing that the industry of the Ruhr will be partially paralysed by the destruction of the three dams.

All were full with the winter and spring rains. Even if repaired within a few months—if such a thing were possible—there would not be enough water to bring them into even partial use again until next spring. It took two years to fill the Sorpe reservoir, the smallest of the three, when it was first constructed.

Some idea of the flood of water released by the destruction of the dams can be judged from the fact that the 202,000,000 tons capacity of the Eder reservoir would have been enough to supply the whole of London for 150 days even in peace time.

The Eder reservoir, near Hemfurth, two miles south of Waldeck, is the largest in Germany. It had a surface area of 4½ square miles.

Its main purpose was to prevent flooding in the Weser and Fulda Valleys in winter and maintain the rivers at navigable depth in summer. It was also used to feed the Ems and Weser Canal and to operte several important power stations.

Kassel, 30 miles below the dam, is mostly low-lying, and its important locomotive works and aircraft factories are gravely threatened.

The half-mile-long Mohne Dam near Soest is 26 miles east of the small manufacturing town of Dortmund, and was built before the last war to confine a reservoir six miles long by two miles wide and holding 134,000,000 tons of water.

It was the biggest source of water for the industries of the Ruhr, the demands of which are enormous. It was largely to meet the needs of the Ruhr's coke ovens and foundries that the dam was built.

The Sorpe Dam lies six miles south of the Mohne Dam, on the Sorpe River, also a tributary of the Ruhr. It was used in conjunction with the Mohne reservoir to control the Ruhr Valley's supplies.

The Daily Telegraph Air Correspondent writes: "Were the mines dropped a little short when the Lancasters were flying towards the dams their forward momentum would carry them against the [illegible]. In any

(Continued on P. 6, Col. 4)

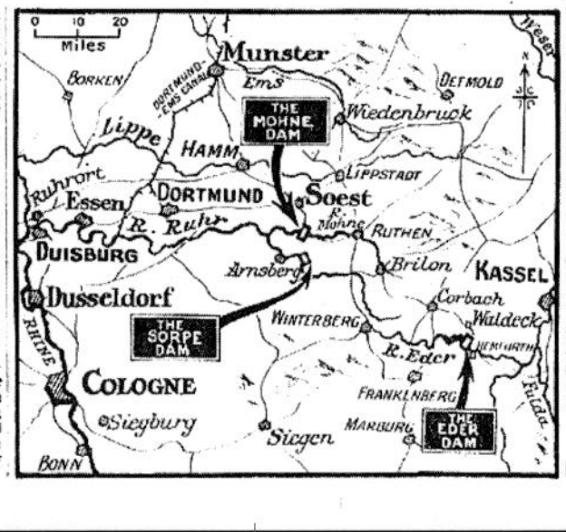

THE MOHNE DAM AFTER THE R.A.F. RAID

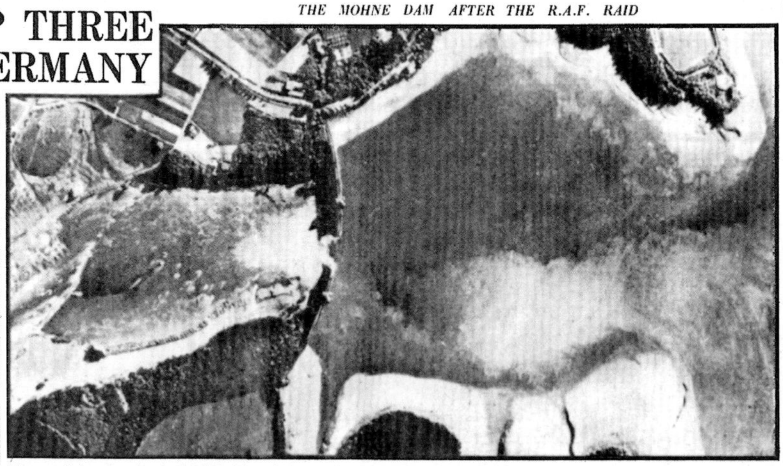

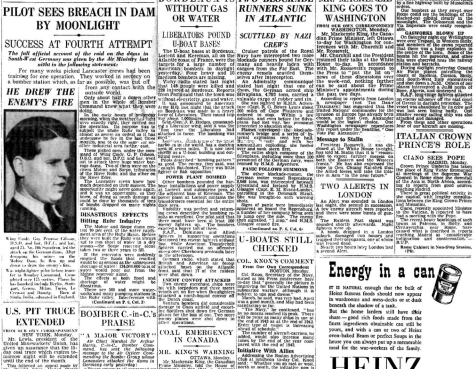

The great Mohne dam after the R.A.F. had done their work and made a breach nearly 300ft wide.

PILOT SEES BREACH IN DAM BY MOONLIGHT

SUCCESS AT FOURTH ATTEMPT

The full official account of the raid on the dams in South-West Germany was given by the Air Ministry last night in the following statement:

For many weeks picked Lancaster crews had been training for one operation. They worked in secrecy on a bomber station which, as far as possible, was cut off from any contact with the outside world.

Only about half a dozen other men in the whole of Bomber Command knew what they were doing.

In the early hours of yesterday morning, when the weather and light were exactly right, they carried out the operation. Its purpose was to subject the whole Ruhr valley to almost as severe an ordeal as it has undergone by fire in the last three months, and to do the same for another industrial area farther east.

These picked men, under the command of Wing Cmdr. G. P. Gibson, D.S.O. and bar, D.F.C. and bar, went out to attack three huge water barrage dams. Two of them were on the rivers Mohne and Sorpe, tributaries of the River Ruhr, and the other on the River Eder.

The Lancaster crews knew how much depended on their success. The opportunity might never come again, and it was an opportunity, as they knew, of doing as much damage as could be done by thousands of tons of bombs dropped on many nights running.

DISASTROUS EFFECTS
Hitting Ruhr Industry

The Mohne and Sorpe dams control 70 per cent. of the water catchment area of the Ruhr Basin. Before they were built the Ruhr was always apt to run short of water in a dry season—the Sorpe reservoir alone takes two or three years to fill.

If the reservoirs were suddenly emptied the floods that resulted would be as serious as the subsequent shortage of water: 134,000,000 tons of water would pour out from the Mohne reservoir alone.

The effects of both flood and shortage of water might be disastrous.

There are 300 and more water-works and many pumping stations in the Ruhr valley. Interference with

(Continued on P. 6, Col. 3)

HE DREW THE ENEMY'S FIRE

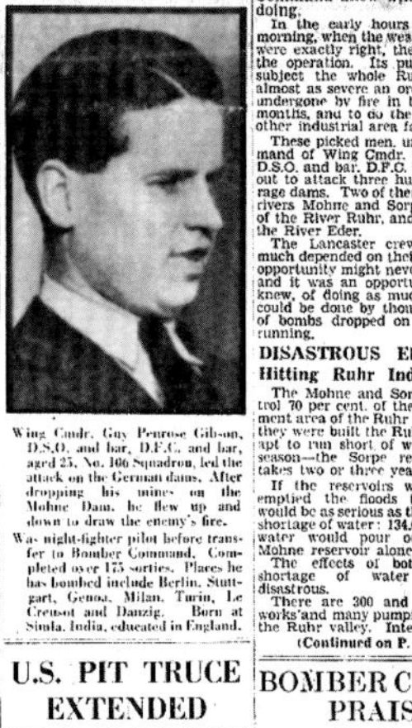

Wing Cmdr. Guy Penrose Gibson, D.S.O. and bar, D.F.C. and bar, aged 25, No. 106 Squadron, led the attack on the German dams. After dropping his mines on the Mohne Dam, he flew up and down to draw the enemy's fire.

Was night-fighter pilot before transfer to Bomber Command. Completed over 175 sorties. Places he has bombed include Berlin, Stuttgart, Genoa, Milan, Turin, Le Creusot and Danzig. Born at Simla, India, educated in England.

U.S. PIT TRUCE EXTENDED

FROM OUR OWN CORRESPONDENT
NEW YORK, Monday.

Mr. Lewis, president of the United Mineworkers' Union, has given an assurance that the 15-day coal truce which expires to-morrow night will be extended until the end of the month.

This followed an appeal made by Mr. Harold Ickes, United States Secretary of the Interior, that work should continue. In this way, he said, "the path will be opened for immediate collective bargaining."

Earlier to-day, the War Labour Board issued a statement on Mr. Lewis's decision not to obey the Board's instruction to attend a meeting to arrange for a renewal of bargaining.

The issue, said the War Labour Board, was "whether Mr. Lewis is above and beyond the laws which apply to all other citizens of the United States." The statement accused Mr. Lewis of "defying the established procedure of the Government," and so "giving aid and comfort to our enemies."

BOMBER C.-in-C.'s PRAISE

"A MAJOR VICTORY"

Air Chief Marshal Sir Arthur Harris, C.-in-C., Bomber Command, has sent the following message to the Air Officer Commanding the Bomber Group whose Lancasters attacked the dams in Germany early yesterday:

"Please convey to all concerned my warmest congratulations on the brilliantly successful execution of last night's operations.

"To the air crews I would say that their keenness and thoroughness in training and their skill and determination in pressing home their attacks will for ever be an inspiration to the Royal Air Force.

"In this memorable operation they have won a major victory in the battle of the Ruhr, the effects of which will last until the Boche is swept away in the flood of final disaster."

LATE NEWS

LONDON ALERTS

(See This Page)

Raiders passed sounded some time afterwards. Later third Alert was sounded.

Enemy aircraft were over South-East England. High-explosive bombs dropped at one coastal town.

"ITALIAN CHIEF OF STAFF RESIGNS"

Moscow radio last night quoted Berne reports that Gen. Ambrosio, Chief of Italian General Staff, had handed resignation to Mussolini, who had asked him to withhold it until the staff had been reorganised.

ROOSEVELT MAY VETO TAX PLAN BILL

Washington, Tuesday.—President Roosevelt is hinting strongly at a veto if Congress approves the modified Income Tax Plan (Pay As You Go) Bill, which has been approved by the Senate.

He declared that he could not acquiesce "in the elimination of whole year's tax burden on upper income groups during a war period."—A.P.

BORDEAUX IS WITHOUT GAS OR WATER

LIBERATORS POUND U-BOAT BASES

The U-boat bases at Bordeaux, Lorient and Kereman, all on the Atlantic coast of France, were the targets for a large number of American bombers in daylight yesterday. Four heavy and 10 medium bombers are missing.

Vichy radio stated last night that 148 people were killed and 228 injured at Bordeaux. Reports from Paris said that the town was without electricity, gas and water.

It was announced by American Army H.Q. last night that the attack on Bordeaux was made by a heavy force of Liberators. Their round trip was about 1,000miles.

Brig.-Gen. J. P. Hodges, commanding a Liberator wing, said it was the "first time the Liberators had attacked in force. The bombing was good."

Bordeaux, which is one of the finest harbours in the world, has a docking area of seven miles. It is now used chiefly as a U-boat building and outfitting centre.

Pilots described "bombing pattern" as good. The enemy, they said, was "caught flat-footed. There was little fighter or flak opposition."

POWER PLANT BOMBED

Other bombers pounded the harbour installations and power supply at Lorient and submarine pens at the adjacent base of Kereman. The power plant at Lorient contains the transformers essential for the entire dock area.

Visibility was perfect and returning crews described the bombing results as excellent. One pilot said that there must have been at least 100 enemy fighters up. The bombers exacted a heavy toll of these.

R.A.F., Dominion and Allied fighters in supporting operations destroyed two enemy fighters without loss, while American Thunderbolt fighters carried out an offensive sweep over Cherbourg peninsula later in the afternoon.

German radio, which stated that British and American air forces attacked bases on the Atlantic front, said that 17 of the raiders were shot down.

ENEMY CONVOY ATTACKED

Two enemy merchant ships were hit with torpedoes and three escort vessels set on fire when Beaufighters attacked a north-bound convoy off the Dutch coast.

Ventura bombers did considerable damage to Caen airfield and escorting Spitfires shot down five German planes for the loss of one. Two more enemy planes were shot down in other operations.

COAL EMERGENCY IN CANADA

MR. KING'S WARNING

OTTAWA, Monday.

Mr. Mackenzie King, the Canadian Prime Minister, told the House of Commons to-day that a national emergency had been declared to exist in the production of coal in Canada.

An order is expected in a few days to compel men with coal mining experience to take employment in mines. Canada faces the possibility of being 4,000,000 tons short of her coal requirements next year.—A.P.

This Morning's War News

Germany
Devastation spreading down Ruhr and Eder valleys after destruction by Lancasters of Mohne, Sorpe and Eder dams; pilots' accounts. (Pp 1 & 6)

Italy
R.A.F. over Rome after moonlight raid on air base. (P1)

France
Heavy day raids on Bordeaux docks and Lorient. (P1)

Sea
Two blockade runners, trapped by Navy, scuttle themselves. (P1)
Atlantic air cover against U-boats now extends almost from port-to-port. (P6)

United States
Mr. Mackenzie King goes to Washington for Churchill-Roosevelt talks. (P1)
Resumption of pit strike threatened as 15-day truce ends. (P1)

Combined Operations
Four hundred Germans killed when destroyer Campbeltown was blown up in St. Nazaire raid. (P3)

Labrador
Allies' huge new air base. (P5)

Tunisia
Navy seizes island off Cap Bon. (P5)

Marshal Messe
Italian C.-in-C. in North Africa arrives in Britain. (P5)

Russia
Russians shelling Sevsk, on south-western base of Germans' Orel salient. (P5)

TWO BLOCKADE RUNNERS SUNK IN ATLANTIC

SCUTTLED BY NAZI CREWS

Cruiser patrols of the Royal Navy have intercepted two more blockade runners bound for Germany and heavily laden with cargoes from the Far East. The enemy vessels scuttled themselves after interception.

An Admiralty communiqué stated last night that one of them, the German armed ship Silvaplana, 4,793 tons, carried a valuable cargo of rubber and tin.

She was sighted by H.M.S. Adventure (Capt. R. G. Bowes Lyon) about 200 miles off Cape Finisterre and ordered to stop. Within a few minutes, and even before the Silvaplana had lost way, her personnel proceeded to abandon ship.

Flames enveloped the blockade-runner's bridge and a series of internal explosions rent her hull. Burning fiercely and with her ammunition exploding, she heeled over and sank stern first.

The entire ship's company of the Silvaplana, including more than 100 personnel of the German navy, were rescued by H.M.S. Adventure.

PANIC FOLLOWS SUMMONS

The other blockade-runner, the German motor vessel Regensburg, 8,068 tons, was intercepted between Greenland and Iceland by H.M.S. Glasgow (Capt. E. M. Evans-Lombe), patrolling in the Denmark Strait. She was brought-to with warning shots.

Signs of panic were immediately apparent on board the Regensburg, a number of her company being seen to jump over the side. The enemy then signalled, "I stop," and H.M.S. Glasgow ceased fire.

(Continued on P. 6, Col. 6)

U-BOATS STILL CHECKED

COL. KNOX'S COMMENT

From Our Own Correspondent
BOSTON, Monday.

Col. Knox, Secretary of the Navy, stated at his Press conference here to-day that "generally the picture is improving for the United Nations in submarine warfare, although it is subject to ups and downs."

March, he said, was very bad. April was a good month, and May had been satisfactory so far.

"The Navy," he continued, "has by no means reached its peak. There will be twice as many ships in use at the end of 1943 as at the end of 1942. Every type of vessel is increasing ahead of schedule."

The number of aircraft-carriers, he added, would also increase many times by the end of the year compared with the end of 1942.

Initiative With Allies

Addressing the Boston Advertising Club at luncheon to-day Col. Knox said: "Whether you go east or west, north or south, the initiative now is in Allied hands."

"When war broke out," he added, "the United States was wondering when the Axis was going to strike next. Come what may now it will be the Allies who will strike, not the Axis."

ATTU BATTLE SATISFACTORY
—Col. Knox

From Our Own Correspondent
WASHINGTON, Monday.

The Navy Department, in one of its shortest communiqués of the war, announced to-night that "operations against the Japanese on Attu Island, in the Aleutians, are continuing."

No further details were given, but Col. Knox, Secretary of the Navy, said in Boston to-day that "the battle was moving along satisfactorily."

The only other indication of its progress was a radio talk last night by a War Department spokesman, Col. Ernest Depuy.

He said that operations were going according to plan on Attu, and that Kiska was next on the agenda.

Earlier to-day Tokyo radio quoted a Japanese army spokesman as saying that the attacking United States forces were landing a steady stream of reinforcements on the island under cover of naval and air bombardment.

GEN. QUINAN

Gen. Sir Edward Pellew Quinan, who was given the command of the new Tenth Army based in Irak and Persia in February last year, has been appointed to the command of the North-Western Army in India.

He succeeds Gen. Sir Cyril Noyes, who, says Reuter, has been compelled to go on leave on account of ill-health.

Black-out (London) 10.33-5.19
Moon rises 7.58 p.m.

MR. MACKENZIE KING GOES TO WASHINGTON

FROM OUR OWN CORRESPONDENT
WASHINGTON, Monday.

Mr. Mackenzie King, the Canadian Prime Minister, left Ottawa to-day for Washington for conferences with Mr. Churchill and Mr. Roosevelt.

Mr. Churchill and the President resumed their talks at the White House to-day. In accordance with Mr. Roosevelt's request to the Press to "put the lid on" news of these discussions over the week-end, nothing further can be said about the Prime Minister's appointments during the past two days.

According to reports from London a newspaper [not The Daily Telegraph] has suggested that the United Nations' commander for the invasion of Europe has already been chosen, and that Gen. Alexander would be the logical choice. One Washington newspaper reproduces this report under the headline, "One Vote For Alexander."

Message to Stalin

President Roosevelt, it was disclosed at the White House to-night, has told M. Stalin that it is "reasonable to expect further success on both the Eastern and the Western fronts." He has also expressed the hope to Gen. Chiang Kai-shek that the Allied forces will take the iniative in Asia "in the near future."

TWO ALERTS IN LONDON

An Alert was sounded in London last night, the second in succession. A few enemy aircraft were reported and there were some bursts of gunfire.

The Raiders Past signal was sounded shortly afterwards. Night fighters were up.

A bomb, dropped in a London suburb, damaged two houses and trapped their occupants, one of whom was feared dead.

Nearly two hours later London had a second Alert.

R.A.F. ATTACK BASE 15 MILES FROM ROME

HANGARS LEFT IN FLAMES

FEEBLE GROUND DEFENCES

From W. E. MUNDY,
Daily Telegraph Special Correspondent
ALLIED H.Q., NORTH AFRICA, Monday.

British Wellington bombers of the North-West African Air Force flew over Rome last night, but dropped no bombs on the city.

They had none to drop. The target for all their bombs was the Italian seaplane base at Lido di Roma, 15 miles south-west of the capital, a few minutes earlier.

So bright was the moon that over Lido di Roma the Wellingtons were able to employ tactics usually associated with speedy daylight fighter-bombers. One made four separate runs over the target, the last being at only 750ft above the ground.

Other Wellingtons, having dropped their bomb loads, swept in twice at altitudes of between 400ft and 500ft to machine-gun planes lined up in front of hangars.

Pilots reported that the burning hangars looked like frameworks of twisted steel.

Axis opposition from ground defences was almost non-existent, and no enemy fighter plane was seen during the whole trip.

Lido di Roma is close to the ancient anchorage of Ostia, at the mouth of the Tiber. It is connected with Rome by a fine highway built by Mussolini's orders.

Our bombers as they swept over Rome could see the buildings of the blacked-out capital clearly in the moonlight. The Colosseum and the Via Imperiale were easily recognisable.

GASWORKS BLOWN UP

On Saturday night our Wellingtons were over Trapani, in Western Sicily, and members of the crews reported that there was a huge explosion in the centre of the town. Some of the bombs hit the gasworks, and other hits were observed near the railway station and barracks.

During daylight yesterday Coastal Air Force planes patrolling the coasts of Sardinia, Corsica, Sicily, and South-West Italy encountered and shot down a Ju.52. Others of our planes intercepted a Ju.88 north of Bone, Algeria, and destroyed it.

R.A.F. long-range fighters attacked an enemy schooner off the east coast of Greece in daylight yesterday. The vessel was abandoned by its crew and was last seen listing badly. One smaller enemy sailing ship was also attacked and damaged.

From these and other operations four of our aircraft are missing.

ITALIAN CROWN PRINCE'S ROLE

CIANO SEES POPE

MADRID, Monday.

Crown Prince Umberto has taken the place of King Victor Emmanuel at meetings of the Supreme War Council in Rome since the downfall of the Axis in North Africa, according to reports from good sources reaching Madrid.

There is great political activity in the capital, with lengthy consultations between the King, Crown Prince and Mussolini.

Ciano, recently appointed Minister to the Vatican, is reported to have had a meeting with the Pope.

The recent heavy bombings of such towns as Palermo, in Sicily, and Civitavecchia, near Rome, have caused what is described in reports reaching Madrid as "considerable indignation and consternation."—B.U.P.

Rome Cabinet in Non-Stop Session, (P6).

CHAPTER 7

The Aftermath

Britain

Harris, Cochrane and Wallis had followed the unfolding drama of the night in the tense atmosphere of the operations room at 5 Group HQ, Grantham. When they received the code word 'Nigger' at 00.56hrs, indicating that the Möhne dam had been breached, followed by 'Dinghy' at 01.54hrs to confirm that the Eder too had been breached, there were scenes of intense jubilation in the ops room as the tension of the night's vigil suddenly evaporated. Wallis, who had paced nervously up and down and buried his face in his hands when each miss was reported, jumped for joy and threw his arms in the air. In his excitement, Cochrane leaped up and shook Wallis firmly by the hand. Harris grabbed

OPPOSITE *The* Daily Telegraph *for Tuesday 18 May 1943. The dams raid makes the front page.* (Author)

LEFT *Safely home, but with adrenalin still pumping through their veins and the look of fatigue etched on their faces, Guy Gibson's crew are debriefed after the raid. As Bomber Harris and Cochrane look on, 617's intelligence officer, Sqn Ldr Townson, unravels the hard facts behind the dramas of the night. From left to right: Harris, Townson, Spafford, Cochrane, Taerum, Trevor-Roper.* (IWM CH9683)

the phone and asked to be put through immediately to Washington, where Churchill and the CAS Sir Charles Portal were attending the Trident Conference. At 04.00hrs a car took Harris, Cochrane and Wallis to Scampton, where they joined the surviving crews of the first wave who were being debriefed.

Once debriefing was over, the crews retired to the mess for bacon and eggs and stood at the bar waiting for the others to arrive. But it eventually became clear that eight aircraft were missing and their crews would not be returning home. Wallis was becoming distressed over the high casualties suffered by the squadron and told Mick Martin if he'd known that so many aircrew were to die, then he'd never have embarked upon the project. Wallis had spent nearly 48 tense hours without sleep and was eventually persuaded to get some rest in Gp Capt Charles Whitworth's house. But the party continued in the mess and around lunchtime transferred to Whitworth's house. Gibson had left early to help the adjutant, Flt Lt Humphries, and 'Chiefy' Powell with the fifty-six casualty telegrams to next of kin. (Three were later discovered to be PoWs.) On the morning of the 18th, the men of 617 Squadron went on some well-earned leave, three days for the ground crews, and seven for aircrew.

Meanwhile, across Britain the news of the raids came as a tremendous fillip to morale. The first reports of the operation were heard on the BBC radio news on the morning of the 17th, and the initial press coverage followed the same day in the regional evening newspapers. It was not until the 18th that the nationals went to town on coverage. 'RAF blow up three key dams in Germany' was the front-page headline in the *Daily Telegraph*, while the *Daily Herald* declared, 'RAF blows up dams with mines: 1,000 ft water spouts'. In a tone of excited triumphalism, the *Telegraph* went on to report:

'With one single blow the RAF has precipitated what may prove to be the greatest industrial disaster yet inflicted on Germany in this war. A force of Lancasters, loaded with mines and with crews specially trained for the task, early yesterday morning attacked and destroyed the great dams on the Möhne and Sorpe rivers, tributaries of the Ruhr, and also the dam on the Eder river. Today walls

of water sweeping down the Ruhr and Eder valleys are carrying everything before them.'

To a blitz-weary nation with little in the way of good news to celebrate since the British victory at El Alamein the previous autumn, this daring raid by RAF Bomber Command deep into the Nazi heartland struck a chord. Post-raid reports and the use of a dramatic photo-reconnaissance picture of the yawning breach in the Möhne dam on the front pages of national newspapers boosted public morale. Obtained at great personal risk by the RAF's high-flying PR Spitfire pilots from Benson, the benefits of selective use of such material as a highly effective propaganda tool soon became apparent to the British government.

News of the attacks provoked a favourable response from Britain's allies overseas, in Soviet Russia, the occupied countries of Europe and in particular the USA. Here it came at a timely point in the Trident Conference, and was widely and positively reported in the media. Up to this point, there were many in North America who had been expressing doubts about the effectiveness of Bomber Command's campaign, as well as that of their own 8th Air

RIGHT *Gibson with an almost complete line-up of 617 Squadron aircrew pictured after the raid (possibly following their investiture on 22 June 1943).* (RAF Museum P4447)

Force. Chastise gave Churchill the propaganda coup he was looking for, and just at the right time.

To 617 Squadron, Operation Chastise was not without its cost in human terms. The operation claimed the lives of fifty-three men, many of whom, like Hopgood, Maudslay and Young, were – even at the tender ages of 21, 21 and 27 respectively – highly experienced bomber pilots and impossible to replace. Sgt Jack Liddell from Weston-super-Mare, who was the rear gunner in the crew of Flt Lt Robert Barlow (AJ-E), was the youngest RAF fatality of the operation. At 18, he must have concealed his true age when he enlisted in 1941.

On 24 May, details of the decorations awarded to 617 Squadron's aircrew were passed on to the squadron, before they were officially announced in the supplement to the *London Gazette* the next day. Gibson received the Victoria Cross: Bomber Harris telephoned him to personally congratulate him on his award. Thirty-three members of the squadron were awarded gallantry decorations in recognition of their part in Chastise, making 617 the most decorated squadron in the RAF.

ABOVE *Outside the officers' mess at Scampton the surviving captains from the raid are caught on camera. Back row, left to right: Flt Sgt Bill Townsend, Flt Lt Joe McCarthy, Flt Lt Harold Wilson (did not fly due to illness in his crew), Wg Cdr Guy Gibson, Flt Lt Les Munro, Flt Lt David Maltby, Flt Sgt Ken Brown. Front row, left to right: Flt Sgt Cyril Anderson, Plt Off Geoff Rice, Flt Lt Harold 'Mick' Martin, Flt Lt David Shannon, Plt Off Les Knight.* **(RAFM P18734)**

PREVIOUS SPREAD
With a scale model of the Möhne dam and two potential designs for the badge of 617 Squadron before him, the King shares a joke with Gibson while Cochrane and Whitworth look on.
(IWM CH9924)

OPPOSITE TOP *The publicity that followed the raid continued unabated, and on 27 May the King and Queen visited Scampton to review 617 Squadron's air and ground crews. With Lancaster G for George as a backdrop (Gibson's aircraft on the raid), Gibson escorts the King.*
(IWM CH9950)

OPPOSITE BOTTOM *Taerum, Trevor-Roper, Maltby, Gibson, Johnson, Martin, Shannon, Hobday and McCarthy are among this happy group of 617 Squadron members outside Buckingham Palace following their investiture.*
(IWM HU62923)

LEFT *Guy Gibson stands crisply to attention for the inspection of 617 Squadron by the King and Queen.*
(IWM TR1002)

ABOVE *Canadian survivors of the dams raid. Of the twenty-nine who took part in the operation, thirteen were killed and one became a PoW. Standing, from left to right: Sgt Stefan Oancia (AJ-F), Sgt Frederick Sutherland (AJ-N), Sgt Harry O'Brien (AJ-N), Flt Sgt Ken Brown (AJ-F), Flt Sgt Harvey Weeks (AJ-W), Flt Sgt John Thrasher (AJ-H), Flt Sgt George Deering (AJ-G), Sgt William Radcliffe (AJ-T), Flt Sgt Don MacLean (AJ-T), Flt Lt Joe McCarthy (AJ-T), Flt Sgt Grant MacDonald (AJ-F). Front, Sgt Percy Pigeon (AJ-W), Plt Off Torger Taerum (AJ-G), Flg Off Danny (Revie) Walker (AJ-L), Sgt Chester Gowrie (AJ-H), Flg Off David Rodger (AJ-T).* (IWM CH9935)

The publicity that followed the raid continued unabated, and on the 27th the King and Queen paid a Royal visit to Scampton, lunching in the officers' mess before being taken on a tour of inspection of aircraft and crews of both 57 and 617 Squadrons. The King also inspected one of 617's Lancasters, complete with Upkeep, and talked to Gibson and several other aircraft captains about their training for the raid and the attack itself.

On 21 June, 617's members travelled to London for their investiture by the Queen (the King was in North Africa) at Buckingham Palace the following day. On the evening of the 22nd, a celebratory dinner was held by A.V. Roe & Co. Ltd, builders of the Lancaster, at the Hungaria Restaurant in Lower Regent Street. In addition to 617 Squadron members, Roy Chadwick, designer of the Lancaster, Barnes Wallis and other personalities from Vickers were also present. The occasion was memorable for many reasons, not least for the fact that the food and drink on the menu were not subject to the usual rationing restrictions.

Guy Gibson achieved celebrity status in the months that followed, although to begin with he was something of a reluctant hero. Morale-boosting visits to war factories across Britain and rousing speeches at Wings for Victory

parades were followed by an invitation from the Prime Minister himself, Winston Churchill, to accompany him to Canada for the Quebec Conference in August. After the conference, there followed a gruelling four-month-long public relations tour of Canada and the USA that saw Gibson attending civic receptions and making speeches at RCAF training airfields. Arriving back in England during December, his first instinct was to return to Scampton and look up his old 'oppoes' on 617 Squadron. But in his absence time had moved on. The squadron was now based at Coningsby and it had a new CO, Wg Cdr Leonard Cheshire. Gibson's hopes of being allowed to return to operations were dashed when 5 Group HQ officially grounded him and posted him away to a job at the Air Ministry in January 1944.

But the Guy Gibson story doesn't end there, as in the months that followed the hero was encouraged to write a book about his experiences as a bomber pilot, eventually to appear as *Enemy Coast Ahead* in 1946. Under the patronage of Winston Churchill, he was selected as the prospective Conservative parliamentary candidate for Macclesfield, but withdrew his candidacy in August, desperate to get back on operations. By now Gibson was an air staff officer at 54 Base and used his position to wangle his way back into operational flying.

OVERLEAF *Australian survivors of the dams raid. Of the thirteen who took part in Chastise, two were killed. From left to right: Flt Lt Bob Hay (AJ-P), Plt Off Lance Howard (AJ-O), Flt Lt David Shannon (AJ-L), Flt Lt Jack Leggo (AJ-P), Plt Off Fred Spafford (AJ-G), Flt Lt Harold Martin (AJ-P), Plt Off Les Knight (AJ-N), Flt Sgt Bob Kellow (AJ-N). Not in this photograph are Plt Off Bert Foxlee and Flt Sgt Thomas Simpson who also survived the raid, and Plt Off Anthony Burcher who became a PoW. (IWM CH9936)*

During their investiture leave, five of 617's twelve Australian aircrew are pictured in an informal pose on the roof of the Admiralty building in London. From left to right: Jack Leggo, Harold (Mick) Martin, Tammy Simpson, Bob Hay and Bert Foxlee. (IWM CH9943)

ABOVE *On 22 June, A.V. Roe & Co. hosted a celebratory dinner at the Hungaria Restaurant on Lower Regent Street in London to mark the investiture of 617's personnel by the Queen. 1) Sir Charles Craven, Chairman, Vickers-Armstrongs; 2) Sir Hew Kilner, Works Manager, Vickers-Armstrongs, Weybridge; 3) Air Cdre John Whitworth, OC RAF Scampton; 4) Flt Lt Les Munro (AJ-W); 5) Capt H.A. 'Sam' Brown, Test Pilot, Avro; 6) Flt Lt 'Capable' Caple, 617 Squadron engineering officer; 7) Flt Sgt Heveron; 8) Flt Lt Harold Wilson; 9) Flt Sgt 'Chiefy' Powell, flight sergeant i/c discipline, 617 Squadron; 10) Flt Lt Dick Trevor-Roper (AJ-G); 11) Flg Off Edward Johnson (AJ-N); 12) Flg Off Harold Hobday (AJ-N); 13) Flt Lt Harry Humphries, 617 Squadron adjutant; 14) Plt Off Don MacLean (AJ-T); 15) Capt Joe 'Mutt' Summers, Chief Test Pilot, Vickers-Armstrongs; 16) Barnes Wallis; 17) Sir Roy Dobson, Managing Director, Avro; 18) Plt Off Lance Howard (AJ-O); 19) Flt Lt Mick Martin (AJ-P); 20) Flt Lt Jack Leggo (AJ-P); 21) Sgt Vivian Nicholson (AJ-J); 22) Flt Lt David Maltby (AJ-J); 23) Flt Lt Joe McCarthy (AJ-T); 24) Wg Cdr Guy Gibson (AJ-G); 25) Flt Sgt Len Sumpter (AJ-L); 26) Plt Off Toby Foxlee (AJ-P); 27) Flt Lt Bob Hay (AJ-P); 28) Flt Sgt Tammy Simpson (AJ-P); 29) Roy Chadwick, Chief Designer, Avro; 30) Sir Frank Spriggs, Chairman, Glosters; 31) Sir Thomas Sopwith, Chairman, Hawker Siddeley. (RAF Museum P4443)*

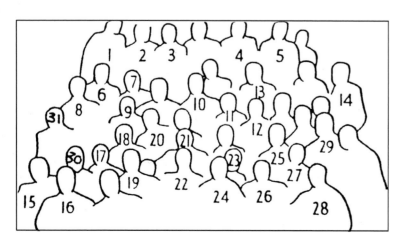

RIGHT *An engaging studio portrait of Guy Gibson taken after the dams raid.* (IWM CH13120)

CONFIDENTIAL.

RECOMMENDATION FOR IMMEDIATE AWARD.

Christian Names .GUY PENROSE............ Surname GIBSON, DSO & Bar., DFC & Bar.

Rank .Squadron.leader.(Acting.Wing... Official No ..39438...........
                    Commander)

Command or Group 5.Group.Bomber.Command Unit ..617.Squadron...........

Total hours flown on operations :   1st Tour (Hampdens)   242.30
                                      2nd Tour (Fighters) NIGHT 199.45
                                      3rd Tour (Lancasters)   200.44

Recognition for which recommended .....Victoria.Cross..............

Appointment held .... Officer Commanding, No. 617 (B) Squadron.

PARTICULARS OF MERITORIOUS SERVICE.

        On joining Bomber Command in the early days of the War, this
then junior Officer quickly established a reputation as an outstanding
operational pilot.   Not content with taking the fullest possible
share in all normal operations, he developed a habit of going out
alone during his "rest" nights to make single-handed attacks on,
for instance, such highly defended objectives as the German battleship "Tirpitz", then completing in Wilhelmshaven.   At the conclusion of his first operational tour on night bombers, he persistently
demanded to remain on operations.   He was, therefore, transferred
to night fighters for his "rest" period, in preference to a training
unit.   At that time the foundations of the night fighter
organization were being laid, and this by then highly experienced
night pilot took a leading part in raising and indoctrinating new
night fighter formations.   During this period as a night fighter
pilot, although stationed in a part of the country comparatively
free from raids, and with night fighting tactics and equipment in
the elementary stage, he destroyed at least three enemy bombers over
this country.   At the conclusion of this tour as a night fighter
pilot, he again insistently demanded to be returned to night bomber
operations.   As a Squadron Commander his second operational tour
on bombers was marked by consistently outstanding achievements, both
as an operational pilot and as the leader of his squadron.   On the
conclusion of this his third operational tour, he again raised the
most strenuous protests against relegation to non-operational duties.
He was therefore given command of a unit then forming for special
tasks.   It was as the Commander of this unit that he led the
attacks on the Moehne and Eder Dams.

        It is typical of this Officer that he himself made the first
attack on the Moehne Dam, thus taking the full brunt of the anti-
aircraft defences while still at their best.   After delivering his
attack with great accuracy from a height of a few feet, he proceeded
to supervise the remainder of the attack on the Moehne Dam.   In the
process he deliberately and repeatedly circled round at a very low
altitude directly over the anti-aircraft defences for 30 minutes
in order to attract their fire to his own aircraft and to enable
his gunners to shoot up the gun positions, thus leaving the remaining
aircraft, which were attacking the Dam in turn, as free as a run as
possible.   After the Moehne Dam had been breached he withdrew
the remainder of his force and led them to the Eder Dam.   Having
already expended his own projectiles, he pursued similar tactics
while the attack on the Eder Dam was successfully developed.
Throughout both attacks he maintained a minute by minute commentary
thus enabling reserve forces to be accurately disposed.

        This young Officer is beyond doubt the most inspiring
leader, efficient operational captain, and outstanding fighting
airman of the Command.   Of a quiet and unassuming manner, and
possessing an unfathomable store of personal courage, he displays
all greatest qualities of leadership including intelligence and
organizing ability of the highest order.   He is as insatiable
in seeking the post of greatest danger as he is imperturbable in
the encounter.

        For extraordinary courage, exceptional leadership and
example in the face of the enemy over three and a half years of
hazardous operations culminating in the successful attacks on
the Moehne and Eder Dams, which he personally led and wherein he
displayed, as is usual with him, the highest valour in the face
of deliberately sought and tremendous additional risk, this
Officer is most strongly recommended for the award of the Victoria
Cross.

CLOCKWISE: *Victoria Cross, Distinguished Flying Cross, Distinguished Flying Medal ribbon, Conspicuous Gallantry Medal ribbon, Distinguished Service Order ribbon.*

LEFT *The official citation for Wg Cdr Guy Gibson's Victoria Cross. (TNA AIR2/4890)*

On 19–20 September 1944 he flew in a 627 Squadron Mosquito as master bomber on a raid against Rheydt and Mönchengladbach. His unfamiliarity with the Mosquito and the marking techniques employed proved to be his undoing, because on the way home his Mosquito crashed in Holland, killing Gibson and his navigator, Sqn Ldr J.B. Warwick. Exactly why they crashed is still a mystery. Perhaps the final words in the Guy Gibson story should be left to his biographer, Richard Morris: 'Gibson died not because he was sent back to battle, but because he refused to be left out of it.'

Following the dams raid, 617 Squadron went from strength to strength. With its reputation for precision bombing it continued to be employed on special bombing tasks until the war's end. Its Lancasters were further modified to carry Barnes Wallis's – 'super bombs' – the 12,000lb Tallboy and latterly the 22,000lb Grand Slam, which were used to breach the Dortmund-Ems Canal, sink the much-feared German battleship *Tirpitz*, and bring down the Arnsberg viaduct, among many other operations. In the 21st century the legend of 617 Squadron lives on, with the Tornado instead of the Lancaster.

OPERATION CHASTISE – Awards to Members of 617 Squadron

Victoria Cross
A/Wg Cdr G.P. Gibson DSO and Bar, DFC and Bar
(OC 617 Squadron and Captain, AJ-G)

Distinguished Service Order
Flt Lt J.C. McCarthy DFC (Captain, AJ-T)
Flt Lt D.J.H. Maltby DFC (Captain, AJ-J)
A/Flt Lt H.B. Martin DFC (Captain, AJ-P)
A/Flt Lt D.J. Shannon DFC (Captain, AJ-L)
Plt Off L.G. Knight (Captain, AJ-N)

Bar to the Distinguished Flying Cross
A/Flt Lt R.C. Hay DFC (Squadron Bombing Leader and B/A, AJ-P)
A/Flt Lt R.E.G. Hutchison DFC (Squadron Signals Leader and
    W/Op, AJ-G)
A/Flt Lt J.F. Leggo DFC (Squadron Navigation Officer and Nav, AJ-P)
Flg Off D.R. Walker DFC (Nav, AJ-L)

Distinguished Flying Cross
A/Flt Lt R.D. Trevor-Roper DFM (R/G, AJ-G)
Flg Off J. Buckley (R/G, AJ-L)
Flg Off L. Chambers (W/Op, AJ-P)
Flg Off H.S. Hobday (Nav, AJ-N)
Flg Off E.C. Johnson (B/A, AJ-N)
Plt Off G.A. Deering (F/G, AJ-G)
Plt Off J. Fort (B/A, AJ-J)
Plt Off C.L. Howard (Nav, AJ-O)
Plt Off F.M. Spafford DFM (B/A, AJ-G)
Plt Off H.T. Taerum (Nav, AJ-G)

Conspicuous Gallantry Medal (Flying)
Flt Sgt K.W. Brown (Captain, AJ-F)
Flt Sgt W.C. Townsend DFM (Captain, AJ-O)

Bar to Distinguished Flying Medal
Sgt C.E. Franklin (B/A, AJ-O)

Distinguished Flying Medal
Flt Sgt G.A. Chalmers (W/Op, AJ-O)
Flt Sgt D.A. MacLean (Nav, AJ-T)
Flt Sgt T.D. Simpson (R/G, AJ-P)
Flt Sgt L.J. Sumpter (B/A, AJ-L)
Sgt D.P. Heal (Nav, AJ-F)
Sgt G.L. Johnson (B/A, AJ-T)
Sgt V. Nicholson (Nav, AJ-J)
Sgt S. Oancia (B/A, AJ-F)
Sgt J. Pulford (FE, AJ-G)
Sgt D.E. Webb (F/G, AJ-O)
Sgt R. Wilkinson (R/G, AJ-O)

PREVIOUS SPREAD
Flt Lt David Shannon meets the King at Scampton.
(IWM CH9953)

ABOVE AND RIGHT
Flt Lt Joe McCarthy (above) and Flt Lt David Maltby (right) meet the King at Scampton.
(IWM CH9925/9)

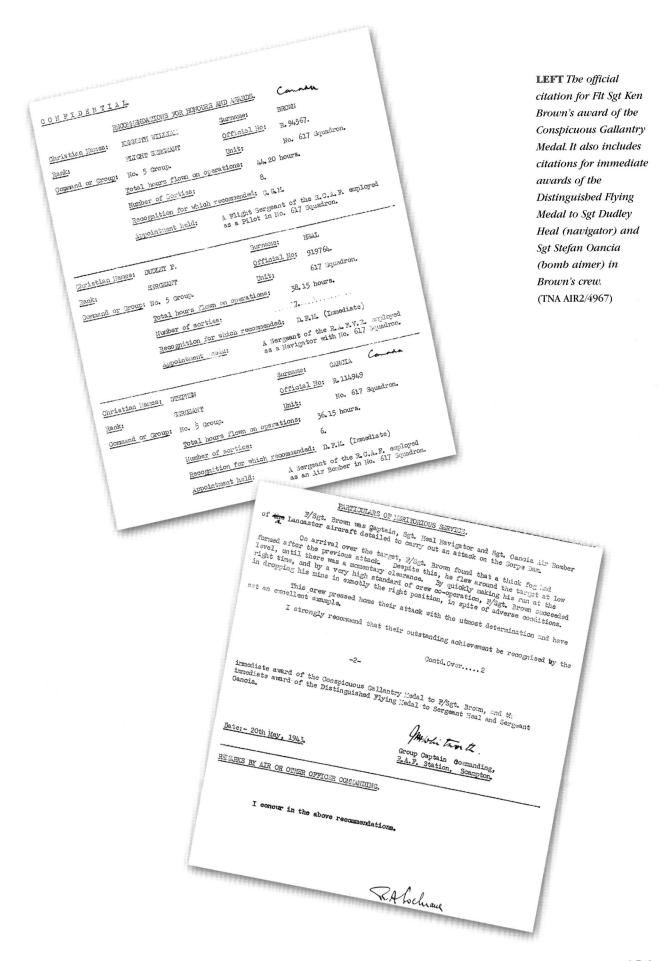

CONFIDENTIAL.

RECOMMENDATIONS FOR HONOURS AND AWARDS.

Canada

Surname: BROWN

Christian Names: KENNETH WILLIAM   Official No: R.94567.

Rank: FLIGHT SERGEANT   Unit: No. 617 Squadron.

Command or Group: No. 5 Group.

Total hours flown on operations: 44.20 hours.

Number of Sorties: 8.

Recognition for which recommended: C.G.M.

Appointment held: A Flight Sergeant of the R.C.A.F. employed as a Pilot in No. 617 Squadron.

Surname: HEAL

Christian Names: DUDLEY P.   Official No: 919764.

Rank: SERGEANT   Unit: 617 Squadron.

Command or Group: No. 5 Group.

Total hours flown on operations: 38.15 hours.

Number of sorties: 7.

Recognition for which recommended: D.F.M. (Immediate)

Appointment held: A Sergeant of the R.A.F.V.R. employed as a Navigator with No. 617 Squadron.

Surname: OANCIA   Canada

Christian Names: STEPHEN   Official No: R.114949

Rank: SERGEANT   Unit: No. 617 Squadron.

Command or Group: No. 5 Group.

Total hours flown on operations: 36.15 hours.

Number of sorties: 6.

Recognition for which recommended: D.F.M. (Immediate)

Appointment held: A Sergeant of the R.C.A.F. employed as an air Bomber in No. 617 Squadron.

PARTICULARS OF MERITORIOUS SERVICE.

F/Sgt. Brown was Captain, Sgt. Heal Navigator and Sgt. Oancia Air Bomber of a Lancaster aircraft detailed to carry out an attack on the Sorpe Dam.

On arrival over the target, F/Sgt. Brown found that a thick fog had formed after the previous attack. Despite this, he flew around the target at low level, until there was a momentary clearance. By quickly making his run at the right time, and by a very high standard of crew co-operation, F/Sgt. Brown succeeded in dropping his mine in exactly the right position, in spite of adverse conditions.

This crew pressed home their attack with the utmost determination and have set an excellent example.

I strongly recommend that their outstanding achievement be recognised by the

Contd. Over.....2

-2-

immediate award of the Conspicuous Gallantry Medal to F/Sgt. Brown, and the immediate award of the Distinguished Flying Medal to Sergeant Heal and Sergeant Oancia.

Date:- 20th May, 1943.

Group Captain Commanding,
R.A.F. Station, Scampton.

REMARKS BY AIR OR OTHER OFFICER COMMANDING.

I concur in the above recommendations.

LEFT *The official citation for Flt Sgt Ken Brown's award of the Conspicuous Gallantry Medal. It also includes citations for immediate awards of the Distinguished Flying Medal to Sgt Dudley Heal (navigator) and Sgt Stefan Oancia (bomb aimer) in Brown's crew.* (TNA AIR2/4967)

CHAPTER 8

Some of the Men Who Made it Happen

Sir BARNES WALLIS (1887–1979)

After the Second World War had ended, Barnes Wallis was awarded the sum of £10,000 for his bomb inventions – Upkeep, Tallboy and Grand Slam. He donated the money to establish an educational foundation for the children of RAF men killed on operations during the war.

The son of a doctor, Barnes Neville Wallis was born on 26 September 1887 in Ripley, Derbyshire. Educated at Christ's Hospital, Sussex, he went on to train as a marine engineer at J.S. White & Co. at Cowes on the Isle of Wight (1905) before being appointed as design draughtsman in the Airship Department of Vickers Ltd (1913). With the outbreak of the First World War, Wallis enlisted in the Artists' Rifles and was later commissioned into the Royal Navy Volunteer Reserve, but in 1916 he was sent back to Vickers to resume his airship design work. From 1923 to 1930 he was Chief Designer of the Airship Guarantee Company and with Sir Dennistoun Burney he worked on the R100 design. Wallis brought a fresh new approach to airship design that utilised his revolutionary 'geodetic' lattice construction principle in their structure. Progressing to heavier-than-air aircraft, Wallis employed geodetics in the design of the single-engine Vickers Wellesley in 1935 followed by the twin-engine Wellington in 1936.

From 1937 to 1945 Wallis was Assistant Chief Designer of the Aviation Section of Vickers-Armstrongs Ltd. With the outbreak of the Second World War his employers and the Air Ministry were keen that he should continue his work on aircraft design and development, but in his spare time he pursued a number of different ideas with which he hoped Britain could defeat the Nazis. Most famous of all his wartime inventions was the revolutionary bouncing

OPPOSITE *Flt Lt Mick Martin (left) and Gp Capt John Whitworth in the presence of the King at Scampton.* (IWM CH9928)

BELOW *Barnes Wallis, designer of the bouncing bomb.* (via Bruce Robertson)

bomb, used to great effect by 617 Squadron to destroy the Möhne and Eder dams in May 1943. Wallis also designed and developed the 12,000lb Tallboy and 22,000lb Grand Slam earthquake bombs that were used to sink the German battleship *Tirpitz* and to destroy vital strategic targets that included U-boat pens and V-weapon sites.

After the war, Wallis continued with his revolutionary designs for aircraft. During his research that began in 1945, he solved the difficult mechanical problem of altering the angle of wing sweep in flight to suit different conditions. Sadly, his ground-breaking work failed to attract the support of the British government and his designs were passed to the USA, and in the mid-1960s they were developed as the General Dynamics F-111 swing-wing bomber.

Wallis was made a CBE in 1943 and knighted in 1968. He was elected FRS in 1945 and was awarded the silver medal of the Royal Aeronautical Society in 1928 and 1937. Wallis maintained a close practical involvement with aviation right up until his death on 30 October 1979, at the age of 92.

Wing Commander GUY GIBSON (1918–44)

Alongside Leonard Cheshire, Guy Gibson is probably the most famous RAF bomber pilot of all time. Precocious, arrogant, and with an unrelenting enthusiasm for operations, he won undying fame for his role leading the attack on the Ruhr dams in May 1943, for which he was awarded the VC. Gibson flew operationally from the day war broke out, completing 177 operational sorties, with few breaks, until his final, fateful flight in September 1944.

Born on 12 August 1918 in Simla, the son of an official in the Imperial Indian Forest Service, Guy Penrose Gibson was educated at St Edward's School, Oxford, before being commissioned into the RAF in 1937. His first posting was to 83 Squadron as a bomber pilot. Gibson's early career in the junior service was undistinguished, but the war

was to bring unforeseen change. Completing his first tour of duty in August 1940, he was posted to instruct at an operational training unit before transferring to Fighter Command and a posting to 29 Squadron flying Bristol Beaufighter night fighter aircraft. In ninety-nine operational sorties Gibson claimed three enemy aircraft destroyed and was promoted to squadron leader with a Bar to his DFC on completion of his second tour in December 1941. A short spell of instructing was followed by a posting back to Bomber Command and the command of 106 Squadron. He completed his second bomber tour in March 1943 as a wing commander, aged 24, with DSO and Bar, DFC and Bar, before he was told to form 617 Squadron on 21 March. He led nineteen Lancasters on the famous dams raid on 16–17 May, in which the Möhne and Eder dams were successfully breached, but eight Lancasters failed to return. Gibson was awarded the VC and remained with the squadron until August, when he was officially taken off operations.

Thereafter and until D-Day, he became a celebrity figure at home and in the USA, a protégé of Winston Churchill, a prospective Conservative Party candidate for Macclesfield, and the author of what later became a best-selling account of the bomber air war, *Enemy Coast Ahead*. However, he was desperate to get back to operational flying and in September 1944 his superiors finally relented and granted him one final sortie. Gibson piloted a 627 Squadron Mosquito as master bomber in a raid on Rheydt and Mönchengladbach on 19 September. On the return journey his aircraft inexplicably flew into the ground and exploded, close to the Dutch town of Steenbergen, killing Gibson and his navigator, Sqn Ldr James Warwick.

Flight Lieutenant 'MICK' MARTIN (1918–88)

'Mick' Martin (see photograph on page 182) was probably the RAF's greatest exponent of low-level bombing, and to those with whom he flew he was the greatest exemplar of low-flying skills, which were

so well demonstrated in the dams raid of 1943. One commentator described him as 'swashbuckling and brave, with scant respect for authority, but with a compelling desire to be at grips with the enemy. But he was highly professional and knew that gallantry was to no avail without skill and tactical sense.'

Born Harold Brownlow Morgan Martin at Edgecliff, New South Wales, on 27 February 1918, 'Mick' Martin was pronounced unfit to fly in Australia because of asthma. Undeterred, he worked his passage to England, where he joined the RAF in 1940. Martin was commissioned in 1941 and then served with 455 Squadron RAAF. He was transferred to 50 Squadron RAF, with whom he flew a further twenty-three sorties before being taken off operational flying and awarded the DFC. Chosen by Guy Gibson to join the newly formed 617 Squadron, Martin flew on the dams raid, for which he was awarded the DSO. Staying with the 'Dam Busters', he became its acting commanding officer and flew on many more dangerous operations until in February 1944 he was grounded by the AOC 5 Group. By this time he had been awarded Bars to his DSO and DFC but was relegated to 'flying a desk' at group headquarters. Frustrated by this turn of events, he managed to inveigle his way back onto operations as the commander of 515 Squadron, flying de Havilland Mosquitos on night intruder and bomber escort sorties. Martin received a second Bar to his DFC and by the war's end he had amassed a total of eighty-three sorties.

On 30 April 1947 he established a record for the flight from London to Cape Town when, flying a Mosquito with Sqn Ldr E.B. Sismore as navigator, he covered the 6,717 miles in 21 hours 31 minutes at an average speed of 310mph.

He was granted a permanent commission in 1945 and enjoyed a highly successful post-war career, rising to high rank. He commanded the 2nd Allied Tactical Air Force and RAF Germany from 1967 to 1970 and retired from the RAF in 1974 as Air Marshal Sir Harold Martin KCB, DSO*, DFC**, AFC. He died on 3 November 1988.

Air Vice-Marshal the Hon. Sir RALPH A. COCHRANE (1895–1977)

In the opinion of AVM Donald Bennett, the legendary commander of 8 (Pathfinder) Group, Cochrane was a disaster: 'He would have been the best group commander in Bomber Command had he done ten trips – or if he had done any trips. But his knowledge of flying and of operations was nil.' Objective truth, or simply the clash of two powerful personalities? Bomber Harris, however, had known Cochrane since before the war and regarded him as 'a most brilliant, enthusiastic and hard working leader of men'.

Born on 24 February 1895, Cochrane was educated at the Royal Naval Colleges at Osborne and Dartmouth before entering the Royal Navy in 1912, transferring to the RAF in 1918. A number of overseas postings culminated in 1936 with his appointment as the first Chief of the Air Staff to the Royal New Zealand Air Force. In 1942, Cochrane became AOC 3 Group Bomber Command, and with the sacking by Harris of AVM Alec Coryton in February 1943 he assumed the command of 5 Group. Cochrane had been a flight commander of a squadron commanded by Bomber Harris in Mesopotamia during the 1920s and as such remained a strong supporter of the C-in-C, a loyalty evidently reciprocated. Nevertheless, Cochrane was a difficult man to get along with and was viewed by many as austere and lacking in humour. He retired from the RAF as Vice-Chief of the Air Staff in 1952, and died in 1977, aged 82.

Air Chief Marshal Sir ARTHUR 'BOMBER' HARRIS (1892–1984)

Known widely by his nickname 'Bomber', but to his aircrews as 'Butch', Air Chief Marshal Sir Arthur Harris was the architect of Britain's strategic air offensive against Germany in the Second World War, and

OPPOSITE *Air Vice-Marshal the Hon. Sir Ralph Cochrane, AOC 5 Group, RAF Bomber Command, 1943.* (IWM CH14564)

he was regarded with affection by his bomber crews, and with awe by his many minions at Bomber Command headquarters.

Although promoted Marshal of the RAF in 1945, unlike the other main leaders of the war years Harris did not receive a peerage in the 1946 New Year honours. Politicians, including Churchill himself, were quick to distance themselves from the bomber offensive once the war had been won, and Sir Arthur Harris and Bomber Command became victims of post-war political expediency.

Group Captain JOHN WHITWORTH (1912–74)

Group Captain John Whitworth was commanding RAF Scampton in 1943 when 617 Squadron was formed there under Wg Cdr Guy Gibson to prepare for the attacks on the Möhne, Eder and Sorpe dams. When the film *The Dam Busters* was made years later, Whitworth was its technical adviser.

Born in Buenos Aires, and educated at Oundle and the RAF College, Cranwell, John Nicholas Haworth Whitworth was in 1936 a flying instructor to Oxford University Air Squadron. Among his pupils was an undergraduate from Merton College called G.L. Cheshire, later to become Gp Capt Cheshire VC, OM.

From the outbreak of the war until September 1943, Whitworth flew on bomber operations, beginning as a squadron leader and finishing as a group captain. He flew over Germany, France, Norway, Italy and Czechoslovakia with 10 Squadron (Whitleys), 78 Squadron (Whitleys and Halifaxes), and 35 Squadron (Halifaxes), the last two of which he commanded. He also flew Lancasters.

In 1948 he became Air Attaché at Bangkok. As Gp Capt (Operations) at Air HQ India, he was responsible for supervising the air evacuation of Europeans from Kashmir after the partition of India. Whitworth was Senior Air Staff Officer, 1 (Bomber) Group, before his appointment as Commandant of the RAF Central Flying School at Little Rissington from June 1958 until he went to Ghana in 1961 as Air Chief of Staff, Ghana Air Force, to supervise

ABOVE *Air Chief Marshal Sir Arthur Harris, Commander-in-Chief RAF Bomber Command, 1942-5.*

OPPOSITE *Group Captain John Whitworth, station commander at Scampton in 1943, pictured here (right) on the set of* The Dam Busters *film in 1954 with Richard Todd.* (Studio Canal)

for three years he pursued the systematic destruction of the Third Reich with a single-minded determination. Of the Allied wartime commanders, Harris is arguably the most controversial, and to this day his name is closely linked with the questionable policy of area bombing. Although he did not invent area bombing, he applied himself rigorously to its execution, and demonstrated to the world the importance of strategic air power and the key role played by the RAF in the Allied war effort.

Harris was a man who expressed himself clearly and who exuded a definite sense of purpose, although he was seen by some as unrefined and rude, lacking in sensitivity, impatient and totally inflexible. Yet generally

the training of the new force. The following year he became AOC, RAF Hong Kong.

Whitworth retired from the RAF as an air commodore, CB, DSO, DFC and Bar. He died on 13 November 1974, aged 62.

Capt JOSEPH J. 'MUTT' SUMMERS (1904–54)

Captain Joe 'Mutt' Summers was Chief Test Pilot at Vickers-Armstrongs, Weybridge, from 1929 to 1951. 'All test pilots regarded him with some awe', wrote Britain's Concorde chief test pilot Brian Trubshaw. 'He was a great pilot who belonged to the "seat of the pants" vintage, a great character, full of humour, as well as being an excellent teacher who was always ready to pass on his vast experience.'

When Summers joined the RAF in 1920 on a short service commission, his abilities as a pilot were soon apparent and led to his posting to the A&AEE at Martlesham Heath in Suffolk, where he test-flew single-seat fighter aircraft. It was there that he acquired the nickname of 'Mutt', by which he became widely known for the rest of his life. In 1929 he was appointed Chief Test Pilot to Vickers and during the course of his service with the company he made more than forty maiden flights in prototype aircraft. On 6 March 1936, Summers played a key part in the birth of an aviation legend when he took up the prototype Spitfire on its maiden flight from the Supermarine airfield at Eastleigh.

During the Second World War he worked closely with Barnes Wallis, testing his bouncing bomb. On 3 December 1942 Summers flew a Wellington bomber for the first test drop of the mine off Chesil Beach on the Dorset coast. Unfortunately the results were not good because the mines shattered on contact with the water, but the trials continued and in January 1943 the weapon finally proved itself.

After the war Summers continued test-flying, and on the thirty-ninth anniversary of Blériot's cross-Channel flight he flew a Nene-engined Vickers Viking airliner from London to Paris in the record time of 34 minutes

7 seconds, at an average speed of 384mph. In 1951, after retiring from test-flying, he was for a year the liaison officer at the Weybridge Division of Vickers-Armstrongs. He was made an OBE in 1946 and a CBE in 1953. 'Mutt' Summers died 6 days after his 50th birthday, on 16 March 1954.

Dr DAVID PYE (1886–1960)

A keen musician and mountaineer, Sir David Randall Pye CB, FRS, MA, ScD, MIMechE, FRAeS, was born in London on 29 April 1886 and educated at Trinity College, Cambridge, where he read mechanical science. During the First World War he served in the RFC and latterly with the RAF as an Experimental Officer before returning to Cambridge in 1919 to become Fellow of Trinity College and lecturer in engineering. In 1925 Pye left the academic world to take up an appointment at the Air Ministry as Deputy Director of Scientific Research, a post he held until 1937, when he became Director. During the early war years he became closely associated with the development of the jet engine, but at the same time he also saw the potential in Barnes Wallis's research to develop an effective method of destroying dams. He offered Wallis his support in 1941, a critical time, sanctioning use of the Road Research Laboratory for a trials programme to assess the effects of explosive charges when placed against or near to a wall of a gravity dam. Pye was knighted in 1952 and was elected President of the Institution of Mechanical Engineers. He died on 20 February 1960.

Dr WILLIAM GLANVILLE (1900–76)

Outstanding both as scientist and director, Sir William Glanville CB, FRS, PhD, ScD, spent all his working life in the scientific civil service.

A physically imposing man of commanding presence, he was not afraid to express his views clearly and firmly. Glanville was widely

When war broke out, he devoted the laboratory to the war effort, and it soon became an important centre of back-room research. Much work was undertaken into recording blast pressures from bombs and other munitions in air and water, and earth movements caused by buried bombs. Extensive use was made of scale models to investigate explosion phenomena as well as the effects on concrete of projectiles and shaped charges. The greatest of these scale-model investigations was to determine the correct position and charges for the attacks on the Möhne and Eder dams.

Glanville was President of the Institution of Civil Engineers in 1950–1, elected FRS in 1958 and knighted in 1960 before he retired in 1965. He died on 30 June 1976.

Sir HENRY TIZARD (1885–1959)

Born on 23 August 1885, educated at Westminster and Magdalen College, Oxford, Henry Thomas Tizard joined the Royal Garrison Artillery on the outbreak of the First World War, transferring to the RFC the following year. By the end of the war he had become lieutenant-colonel and Assistant Controller of Experiments and Research for the fledgling RAF. Later, during the Second World War, in his role as Chairman of the Aeronautical Research Committee and Scientific Adviser to the Chief of the Air Staff, his influence was vital in securing for Barnes Wallis the use of the shipping research tanks at the National Physical Laboratory in Teddington. Sir Henry Tizard GCB, AFC, FRS, died on 9 October 1959.

Air Marshal Sir CHARLES PORTAL (1893–1971)

A quiet and affable man, the 46-year-old 'Peter' Portal was still relatively young to succeed Sir Edgar Ludlow-Hewitt as C-in-C Bomber Command in 1940, but his prodigious intelligence and determination as a commander had singled him out for high office. Just six months into his command at High Wycombe

respected for his intellect and powers of judgement, as well as for his loyalty to his staff.

Born in London on 1 February 1900, the son of a builder, he was educated at Kilburn Grammar School and the University of London. He graduated in 1922 with a First Class Honours degree in civil engineering and began work as an engineering assistant at the newly formed Building Research Station, initially at Acton, and then at Garston near Watford. His main contribution in research was his early work on the properties of reinforced concrete, which ultimately formed the basis for a code of practice for the design of reinforced concrete structures.

he was appointed Chief of the Air Staff in October 1940, in which role he was later to become strongly committed to using Bomber Command in the fullest way possible to destroy Nazi Germany.

An authority on falconry and fishing, Charles Portal was born on 21 May 1893 and educated at Winchester and Christ Church, Oxford. He joined the Royal Engineers in 1914 and as a corporal was mentioned in despatches before receiving a commission and transferring to the RFC as an observer. By the end of the First World War he had risen to the rank of lieutenant-colonel, with a DSO and Bar, and an MC. Between the wars his RAF career was

meteoric and during his short spell at the helm of Bomber Command he steered it through the dangerous summer of 1940. He took office as Chief of the Air Staff that same year, where he remained for the duration of the war.

Portal was a member of the Chiefs of Staff Committee, in which capacity he played a full part in presenting to the Prime Minister and the War Cabinet the advice of the Chiefs of Staff on Allied strategy and other important matters of military policy. He was also present at all the wartime conferences of the Allied leaders, including Trident in Washington (where he was on the night of the dams raid). He died on 22 April 1971.

ABOVE *Air Marshal Sir Charles Portal, Chief of the Air Staff, 1940-5.*

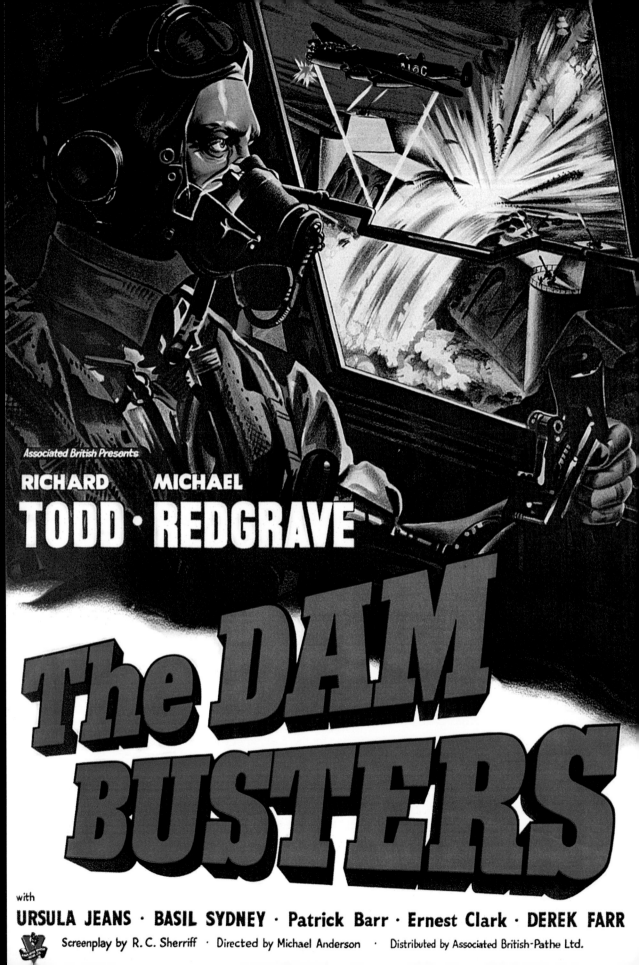

CHAPTER 9

A Cinematic Legend

MAKING *THE DAM BUSTERS* FILM

With the defeat of the Axis powers in 1945, six years of bitter fighting came to an end. A whole host of personal war stories were just waiting to be told, and it was not long before the first of the auto-biographies by the RAF's wartime high commanders and squadron bosses hit the bookstalls. Wing Commander Guy Gibson's classic, *Enemy Coast Ahead*, was published posthumously in 1946 (spawning Paul Brickhill's equally good *The Dam Busters* in 1951), closely followed in 1947 by Marshal of the RAF Sir Arthur Harris's *Bomber Offensive* and Air Vice-Marshal Donald Bennett's *Pathfinder* (1958).

Not to be outdone, the film-makers made a significant contribution to the wartime lore of the RAF. Terence Rattigan's *The Way to the Stars* (1945) and Philip Leacock's *Appointment in London* (1953) highlighted on the big screen the part played by the men of Bomber Command during the war years. But, arguably, one of the most famous of all British war films must be *The Dam Busters*, combining stiff-upper-lip performances, British design ingenuity and strong storyline in full measure.

Eleven years after the dams raid, 617 Squadron's remarkable exploit was turned into a blockbusting film by the Associated British Pictures Corporation (ABPC), starring Michael Redgrave as Barnes Wallis and Richard Todd as Guy Gibson. To this day it has remained one of the most enduring war films of all time, thanks in part to the understated way in which the story is told. But this was not the first time a film had been proposed about the raid: late in 1943 an American proposal to make a Hollywood movie about the dams raid was considered by the Air Ministry and the Ministry of Information. However, British reluctance to divulge specific operational details to the Hollywood studio, not to mention strong criticism of the script from, among others, Barnes Wallis, meant the plan came to nothing.

The screenplay for ABPC's picture was by the famous British playwright R.C. Sherriff, author of *Journey's End* and the screenplay for the movie *The Invisible Man*. It was based on the first half of Paul Brickhill's best-selling book, *The Dam Busters*, and on a part of Gibson's own account in *Enemy Coast Ahead*. Michael Anderson, who was relatively unknown in the film world at the time, was picked to direct the film. It was his first major picture, although he was later to win acclaim for directing *The Quiller Memorandum*, *Around the World in Eighty Days* and *Logan's Run*. He chose to approach the story in a documentary style and to film it in monochrome, thereby giving the story a hard-edged grittiness that colour stock would have failed to do. It also enabled original film footage of bouncing bomb test drops made during the war to be seamlessly inserted into the new feature film. When Eric Coates was

OPPOSITE Cinema poster advertising Michael Anderson's The Dam Busters. *(Studio Canal)*

PAN-Books

ENEMY COAST AHEAD
Guy Gibson V.C.

Illustrated GREAT PAN volume

PAN-Books

THE DAM BUSTERS
Paul Brickhill

Illustrated GREAT PAN volume   2'6

ABOVE *Inspirations for a cinema epic: Guy Gibson's* Enemy Coast Ahead *(1946), and Paul Brickhill's* The Dam Busters *(1951).*

approached to write the title theme, he replied, 'I think I finished it yesterday.' In fact, he had already written a suitable work, and his rousing 'Dam Busters March' became one of the best-known pieces of film music ever written. It made the Top Ten in 1955, remained there for more than a year and was even arranged as a hymn tune.

To make the film as accurate as possible, when work on the script began in earnest, drafts were sent to aircrew survivors of the dams raid for their comments. Expert technical advice was also on hand from Barnes Wallis himself (he paid many visits to Elstree Studios during the film's production), as well as from

'Bomber' Harris, the Hon. Sir Ralph Cochrane (AOC 5 Group in 1943), Mick Martin (skipper of P for Popsy) and Gp Capt J.N.H. Whitworth (station commander at Scampton in 1943).

For many, the star of the film is undoubtedly the Avro Lancaster itself. It is hard to believe that Lancasters were in short supply in April 1954 when filming commenced at RAF Scampton, but four Mk 7 aircraft were taken out of storage from 20 Maintenance Unit, Aston Down, and specially modified for the film: these were NX673, NX679, NX782 and RT686. In fact, 673, 679 and 782 had already developed a

Upkeep was still on the secret list when The Dam Busters *was made, and it remained so until 1973. For the purposes of the film, an accentuated representation of the bouncing bomb was fabricated and bolted to the underside of the Lancasters. Also visible in this photograph is the cut-away bomb bay.* (Studio Canal)

RIGHT *Lancaster NX679 was the only one of the four Lancasters that had its serial number altered for the film. It became Guy Gibson's AJ-G/ ED932.*

OVERLEAF *Close-formation flying was demanded by the film's director, Michael Anderson, and by the director of photography, Erwin Hillier.* (Mike Cawsey/ Garbett & Goulding Collection)

taste for the movies because they had recently starred in Philip Leacock's feature film about a wartime Lancaster squadron, *Appointment in London*, which was premiered in 1953.

In common with the actual Lancaster B Mk III (Type 464 Provisioning) that flew on the dams raid in 1943, three of the Mk 7s (NX673, NX679 and RT686) had their mid-upper gun turrets and bomb bay doors removed to convert them to the authentic dam buster configuration. The bomb bay itself was further modified to create the rebated aperture from which the mock-up of the bouncing bomb was suspended. However, the bomb itself was still on the secret list when the film was being made, so the resulting mock-up bore little resemblance to the real thing.

The aircraft wore different squadron code letters on each side of the fuselage, thereby enabling three Lancasters to play the parts of six on screen. NX679 was painted to represent Guy Gibson's ED932 AJ-G, and it was the only aircraft to have its serial number altered for the film. The other Lancasters retained their official RAF serials. NX673 was painted in the markings of Mick Martin's P for Popsy. One Lancaster, NX782, was retained as a standard Mk 7, and painted as ZN-G to represent Gibson's aircraft when he served with 106 Squadron, before being called upon to form 617 Squadron.

Another aircraft that had a 'walk-on' role in the film was Vickers Wellington T10, MF628, which appears briefly in the early part of the film on a test air-drop of the mine. Because her appearance on screen was short, it was decided to keep MF628 in her silver Training Command livery instead of repainting her in the standard wartime night bomber camouflage of black, dark green and dark earth. At the time of filming in 1954, MF628 was the only flying example of the Wellington extant, and today she can still be seen on static display at the RAF Museum, Hendon.

The RAF put Scampton aerodrome at the disposal of ABPC for the principal location work, and a spell of good weather meant filming could proceed unhindered, starting in April 1954. Avro Lincoln crews from 83 and 97 Squadrons at nearby RAF Hemswell flew the Lancasters on camera. Led by Ken

RIGHT *Flt Lt Ken Souter was chief pilot on the film.* (Ken Souter)

BELOW *Some of the Avro Lincoln crews who flew the Lancasters during the making of the film.* (Garbett & Goulding Collection)

Souter, who had flown Hawker Hurricanes operationally during the war, the crew captains who flew the Lancasters on film were Joe Kmiecik (also a former fighter pilot, on Spitfires and Mustangs), Ted Szuwalski, Dick Lambert and Eric Quinney. Under the control of director of photography Erwin Hillier, much of the superb aerial footage was filmed by ABPC's second unit team from a loaned RAF Vickers Varsity and from the Wellington. To facilitate filming, the metal floor of the Varsity was replaced by a wooden one, to which was attached camera tripods and grips. The aircraft's nose section was also modified to take a forward-looking camera. A further two cameras were installed inside the aircraft, one beside the rear port side passenger access door and the other in the left-hand seat of the cockpit, the pilot flying from the right-hand seat.

For reasons of authenticity, the former Fighter Command airfield at Kirton-in-Lindsey was used for some filming because its grass runway resembled wartime Scampton. Flying sequences showing the early tests of the bouncing bomb were shot off the shoreline at Skegness in Lincolnshire because it was near to the main filming activity at Scampton. The practice flights before the raid, and the actual bombing runs over the dams during the raid itself, were filmed over Lake Windermere in the Lake District and at the Derwent reservoir and dam in the Derbyshire Peak District. In fact, the latter was one of three dams actually used by 617 Squadron in April and May 1943 for intensive flying training before the raid.

BELOW *Flight engineers and pilots. Left to right: Mike Cawsey, Jock Cameron, Joe Kmiecik and Ted Szuwalski. (*Garbett & Goulding Collection)

PREVIOUS SPREAD
When The Dam
Busters *was filmed
at RAF Scampton in
1953–4, the station
had changed little
since the war. Here,
617's crews are filmed
leaving from the actual
building at Scampton
where the final
operational briefing
took place in 1943.*
(Studio Canal)

RIGHT *During
training for the
actual dams raid,
Henry Maudslay
returned from a low-
level training sortie
with foliage caught
on the underside of
his Lancaster. Here,
Richard Todd as Guy
Gibson, Nigel Stock
(Fred Spafford) and
Brewster Mason (Dick
Trevor-Roper) look
on as a similar scene
is recreated during
filming.* (Studio Canal)

Michael Redgrave as Barnes Wallis, during filming at the National Physical Laboratory's Ship Tank at Teddington, where tests for the bouncing bomb were recreated for the film. (Studio Canal)

Harbingers of destruction: Lancasters stand bombed-up and ready for take-off in the film. (Studio Canal)

Scenes of the Lancasters crossing the 'enemy coast' were shot over Gibraltar Point near Skegness. The scenes of inundation in the Ruhr Valley that appear towards the end of the film were photographed in 1954 when the area of the dams itself fell victim to a natural flood disaster. Michael Anderson sent a film unit to Germany especially to capture this event for incorporation into the final version of the film. Camera crews also filmed at a number of other locations in England that included the National Physical Laboratory at Teddington, and the Building Research Station at Garston, near Watford – both of which were the locations for the original tests connected with the dams raid.

Once the location filming had been completed in September, the unit moved to ABPC's studios at Elstree in Hertfordshire, where the set builders and model makers had been hard at work. The office interiors for Bomber Harris, Gibson and Wallis had been recreated, as well as a number of interiors at Scampton and the 5 Group operations room. Although the real 5 Group underground operations room at Grantham had been sealed

BELOW *Inside 5 Group's operations room at Grantham, the tension mounts as Operation Chastise reaches its climax. The ops room was accurately recreated for the film from photographs and plans of the original building. Left to right: Basil Sydney as Harris, Michael Redgrave (Wallis), Derek Farr (Whitworth), and Ernest Clark (Cochrane).* (Studio Canal)

up at the end of the war, by a stroke of luck it had remained untouched since then, its contents frozen in time. ABPC had discovered this fact and were allowed in to photograph this remarkable time capsule, thereby enabling them to recreate a faithful studio mock-up for the film.

For the various scenes depicting action inside the Lancasters, ABPC constructed mock-ups at Elstree of the various crew stations, as well as installing a complete Lancaster nose section mounted on a moving platform. The cockpit controls were linked to a motor beneath the platform to create a kind of basic flight simulator. When the control column was moved the platform moved too, creating a realistic flying movement of the aircraft nose section on screen.

During the long spells of filming in the studio, Richard Todd was strapped into the pilot's seat in the nose section for hours at a time while scenes were shot and shot again until the director was happy with the result. To help pass the time in between 'takes', Todd was taught by an RAF flying instructor how to 'fly' the platform correctly, learning how to operate a Lancaster up to take-off speed. For the purposes of the film, he had to be seen starting up and taxiing, and on occasions he actually piloted a Lancaster on its take-off run at speeds of up to 70mph. Sadly for Todd, he then had to throttle back the engines and return to the dispersal.

To simulate the explosions of the bouncing bombs and the dam walls crumbling away under the massive back-pressure of water, it was important to recreate authentic scale models of the dams and their lakes in the studio. Three accurate mock-ups of the dams and surrounding countryside, measuring 300ft long by 150ft wide, filled the entire sound stage at Elstree. Camera tracks and a swinging arm for the high-speed camera were also added to facilitate filming.

It took ten months of filming before the picture was finally 'in the can' and post-production work could commence. The film then had to be edited, special effects incorporated and the soundtrack added.

Demand for tickets to see the première of *The Dam Busters* was so great that two Royal

Performances were held in London. The first showing on 16 May 1955 – the twelfth anniversary of the raid – was attended by Princess Margaret. Also present were some of the surviving aircrew from the dams raid, including Mick Martin (skipper AJ-P), Harold Hobday (navigator AJ-N) and Bert Foxlee (front gunner AJ-P), as well as Guy Gibson's father, and his widow, Eve. The second performance on the following night was screened in the presence of the Duke and Duchess of Gloucester.

Once filming had been completed, in October 1954 the four Lancasters that helped to recreate the epic story were returned to the RAF maintenance unit at Aston Down, where they languished until declared surplus to requirements. Without ceremony, they were sold to the British Aluminium Co. in July 1956 and melted down for scrap.

To this day the film *The Dam Busters* remains a classic of its kind and a fitting memorial to the achievements of Barnes Wallis, Guy Gibson and the gallant men of 617 Squadron. However, it is sad to report that for reasons of political correctness, a television showing of *The Dam Busters* by ITV in June 2001 saw all references to Guy Gibson's black Labrador dog, 'Nigger', expunged from the film. When challenged on the matter, a spokesman for ITV said that the word 'nigger' was offensive and that they didn't want to upset viewers. It is a fact that the word 'nigger' is offensive to many people in the 21st century, but the film and Guy Gibson's decision to name his dog as he did were products of their time – a different world with a different set of values. This rewriting of history to suit the mood of the day is a dangerous road to go down, and one cannot help but ask just how far we should go in distorting historical fact to conform to the whim of the moment.

Thankfully, there were people during the Second World War years who were prepared to speak frankly, defend freedom of speech and even sacrifice their lives; certainly, without such sacrifice, the rewriting of history to suit political ideology would have become commonplace in the totalitarian society that a Nazi-dominated Britain would have become.

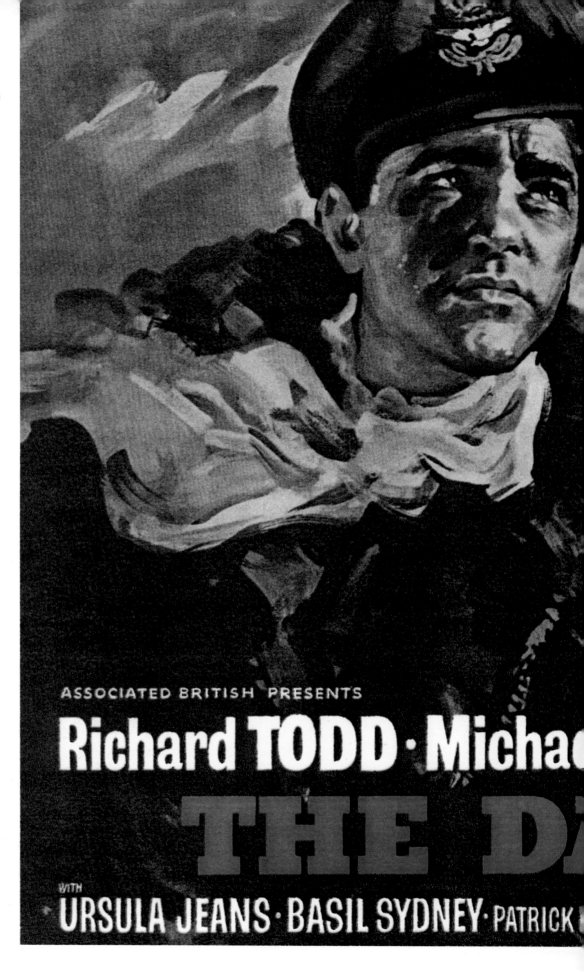

PREVIOUS SPREAD
Richard Todd as Guy Gibson is told that his black Labrador dog, Nigger, has been run over and killed outside the camp gates.
(Studio Canal)

RIGHT *The cover of the souvenir programme produced for* The Dam Busters.
(Studio Canal)

ASSOCIATED BRITISH PRESENTS

Richard TODD · Micha

WITH

URSULA JEANS · BASIL SYDNEY · PATRICK

REDGRAVE in

M BUSTERS

R · ERNEST CLARK AND DEREK FARR

SCREENPLAY BY R.C. SHERRIFF
DIRECTED BY MICHAEL ANDERSON
Distributed by Associated British-Pathe

Mission accomplished: Richard Todd (Gibson) and his crew on arriving back at Scampton after Operation Chastise. Lancaster Mk 7, NX679, was the only aircraft to have its serial altered for the film when it was painted to represent Guy Gibson's Lancaster, ED932/AJ-G. NX679 had also featured in another film about a wartime Lancaster bomber squadron, Appointment in London, *in 1952. (Studio Canal)*

The Aircraft in the Film

Avro Lancaster
Built in 1945 by Austin Motors, Longbridge, as B Mk VIIs

NX673
Sept 1945	Issued to 32 MU (RAF St Athan)
Nov 1945	To 9 Squadron, RAF Waddington
Jan 1946	To India for photo survey work
Apr 1946	Returned to UK. Stored at 20 MU (RAF Aston Down)
Mar 1950	To 5 MU (RAF Kemble)
Apr 1950	Returned to 20 MU
May 1952	Issued out for film work at RAF Upwood (*Appointment in London*)
Jul 1952	To 20 MU
Mar 1954	To RAF Hemswell for filming (*The Dam Busters*). Painted in the markings of Flt Lt Mick Martin's AJ-P
Oct 1954	Returned to 20 MU and declared non-effective stock
Jul 1956	Scrapped

NX679
Jul 1945	To 617 Squadron RAF Waddington
Oct 1945	Issued to 32 MU
Jan 1946	To India
May 1952	Returned to UK and stored at 20 MU, issued out for film work at RAF Upwood (*Appointment in London*)
Jul 1952	Returned to 20 MU
Sept 1953	Transferred to non-effective stock
Mar 1954	To RAF Hemswell for filming (*The Dam Busters*). Painted to represent Wg Cdr Guy Gibson's AJ-G/ED932, the only one of the four Lancasters to have its serial altered for the film
Oct 1954	Returned to 20 MU and declared non-effective stock
Jul 1956	Scrapped

NX782
Oct 1945	Unspecified ground accident, Cat Ac
Mar 1946	With Air Command South East Asia, probably with Tiger Force
May 1946	Issued for return to UK
May 1952	Issued out for film work at RAF Upwood (*Appointment in London*)
Jul 1952	Held at 20 MU
Mar 1954	To RAF Hemswell for filming (*The Dam Busters*). Retained as standard Mk 7 to represent Wg Cdr Guy Gibson's aircraft ZN-G when CO of 106 Squadron
Oct 1954	Returned to 20 MU and declared non-effective stock
Jul 1956	Scrapped

RT686
	Issued to 32 MU
Feb 1946	To RAF Swinderby
Mar 1946	To 15 MU (RAF Wroughton)
Sept 1953	Transferred to non-effective stock
Mar 1954	To RAF Hemswell for filming (*The Dam Busters*)
Oct 1954	Issued to 20 MU and declared non-effective stock again
Jul 1956	Scrapped

(Lancaster histories compiled by Trevor Green, with additional research by the author)

Vickers Wellington
Built in 1944 as a B Mk X by Vickers (Blackpool)

MF628
May 1944	Issued to 18 MU, RAF Tinwald Downs
Mar 1948	Converted to T10 by Boulton Paul, Wolverhampton
Apr 1949	To No 1 Air Navigation School, RAF Hullavington
Dec 1951	Accidental damage (Cat 4), but repairable
Oct 1952	To 19 MU RAF St Athan
Apr 1954	To RAF Hemswell for use in filming of *The Dam Busters*
1955	Sold to Vickers-Armstrongs, Weybridge
1956	Presented to Royal Aeronautical Society
1972	On permanent loan to RAF Museum
1981	Returned to original B Mk X configuration

Lancaster NX679, wearing the squadron codes of Gibson's G for George, captured by the camera at low level over Lincolnshire during filming.
(Mike Cawsey/Garbett & Goulding Collection)

APPENDIX 1

Failed to Return

Eight 617 Squadron crews failed to return from the dams raid, representing the loss of fifty-six aircrew, of whom only three men survived to become prisoners of war. The circumstances of each aircraft loss are recorded below, and the individual aircrew names that follow include details of rank, decorations, age, and home town (where known) at the time of death. Also included are details of the three prisoners of war and the three aborted sorties.

THE CASUALTIES

Hopgood crew

AJ-M, ED925/G damaged by flak on its approach to Möhne dam, then caught in the blast from its Upkeep weapon which had overshot the parapet and exploded on the air side of the dam. Crashed at 00.34hrs at Ostonnen, 3¾ miles east of Werl, Germany.

Flt Lt John Vere Hopgood DFC and Bar, RAFVR, 21 (Seaford, Sussex)
Sgt John William Minchin RAFVR, 27 (Bedford)
Sgt Charles Brennan RAFVR
Flg Off Kenneth Earnshaw RCAF
Plt Off George Henry Ford Goodwin Gregory DFM, RAFVR

Young crew

AJ-A, ED877/G shot down by flak crossing the Dutch coast on the return flight, and crashed at 02.58hrs off Castricum-aan-Zee, Holland.

Sqn Ldr Henry Melvin Young DFC and Bar, RAFVR, 27
Sgt David Taylor Horsfall RAF, 23 (Hove, Sussex)
Sgt Lawrence William Nichols RAFVR, 33 (Westgate, Kent)

Flg Off Vincent Sanford MacCausland RCAF, 30
(Prince Edward Island, Canada)
Sgt Gordon Arthur Yeo RAFVR, 20 (Barry Dock,
S. Wales)
Sgt Wilfred Ibbotson RAFVR, 29 (Bretton West,
Yorks)
Flt Sgt Charles Roberts RAFVR

Maudslay crew
*AJ-Z, ED937/G badly damaged over the Möhne
dam by the detonation of its own Upkeep
weapon and hit by flak on the return flight.
Crashed at 02.36hrs at Netterden, 1¾ miles east
of Emmerich, Germany.*
Sqn Ldr Henry Eric Maudslay DFC, RAFVR, 21
(Broadway, Worcs)
Sgt John Marriott DFM, RAFVR, 23 (Chinley,
Cheshire)
Flg Off Robert Alexander Urquhart DFC, RCAF
WO2 Alden Preston Cottam RCAF, 30 (Jasper
Park, Alberta)
Plt Off Michael John David Fuler RAFVR, 23
(West Wickham, Kent)
Flg Off William John Tytherleigh DFC, RAFVR,
21 (Hove, Sussex)
Sgt Norman Rupert Burrows RAFVR

Astell crew
*AJ-B, ED864/G flew into high-tension cables
and pylon on the outward flight near Marbeck,
3 miles SSE of Borken, Germany. Crashed at
00.15hrs.*
Flt Lt William Astell DFC, RAFVR, 23 (Manchester)
Sgt John Kinnear RAF, 21 (East Newport, Fife)
Plt Off Floyd Alvin Wile RCAF, 24 (Truro, Nova
Scotia)
WO2 Abram Garshowitz RCAF
Flg Off Donald Hopkinson RAFVR, 22 (Royton,
Lancs)
Flt Sgt Francis Anthony Garbas RCAF
Sgt Richard Bolitho RAFVR, 23 (Portrush, Co.
Antrim)

Barlow crew
*AJ-E, ED927/G flew into high-tension cables on
the outward flight at Haldern, 2½ miles ENE of
Rees, Germany. Crashed at 23.50hrs.*
Flt Lt Robert Norman George Barlow DFC,
RAAF, 32 (St Kilda, Victoria)
Plt Off Samuel Leslie Whillis RAFVR, 31
(Fenham, Newcastle-upon-Tyne)

Flg Off Philip Sidney Burgess RAFVR, 20

Flg Off Charles Rowland Williams DFC, RAAF,
34 (Torrens Creek, Queensland)

Plt Off Alan Gillespie DFM, RAFVR, 20
(Carlisle)

Flg Off Harvey Sterling Glinz RCAF, 22
(Winnipeg, Manitoba)

Sgt Jack Robert George Liddell RAFVR, 18
(Weston-super-Mare, Som.)

Byers crew

*AJ-K, ED934/G hit by flak on the outward
flight from batteries on the Dutch
island of Texel and crashed into the
Waddenzee west of Harlingen (precise time
unknown).*

Plt Off Vernon William Byers RCAF, 32
(Codette, Saskatchewan)

Sgt Alastair James Taylor RAF, 20 (Alves,
Moray)

Flg Off James Herbert Warner RAFVR

Sgt John Wilkinson RAFVR, 21 (Antrobus,
Cheshire)

Plt Off Arthur Neville Whitaker RAF

Sgt Charles McAllister Jarvie RAFVR, 21
(Glasgow, Scotland)

Flt Sgt James McDowell RCAF

Ottley crew

*AJ-C, ED910/G hit by flak on the outward flight
and crashed on the Boserlagerschenwald near
Hessen, 1¾ miles NNE of Hamm, Germany, at
02.35hrs.*

Plt Off Warner Ottley DFC, RAFVR

Sgt Ronald Marsden DFM, RAF, 23 (Redcar,
Yorks)

Sgt Harry John Strange RAFVR, 20 (Holloway,
London)

Flt Sgt Thomas Barr Johnston RAFVR (Bellshill,
Lanarks)

Sgt Jack Guterman DFM, RAFVR, 23 (Guildford,
Surrey)

Flg Off Jack Kenneth Barrett DFC, RAFVR, 22
(Goodmayes, Sussex)

Burpee crew

*AJ-S, ED865/G hit by flak on the outward flight
and crashed at 02.00hrs near Gilze-Rijen
airfield, Holland.*

Plt Off Lewis Johnstone Burpee DFM, RCAF, 25
(Ottawa, Ontario)

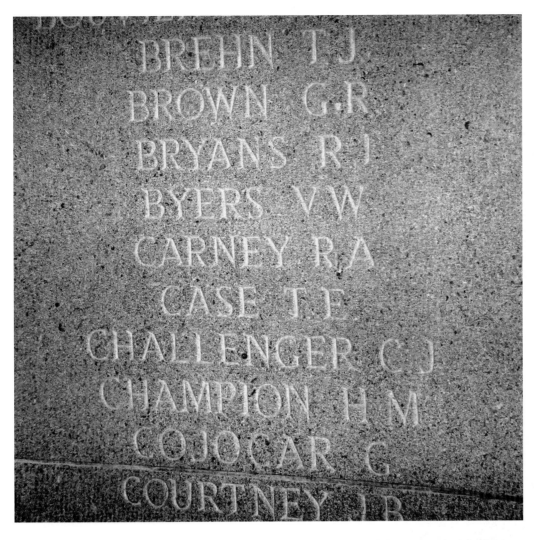

LEFT *The Lancaster of Plt Off Vernon Byers (AJ-K) was hit by flak on the way to the dams and crashed into the Waddenzee off the Dutch coast. His name is commemorated on the Commonwealth Air Forces Memorial at Runnymede in Surrey, together with most of his crew and 20,000 other Commonwealth airmen who have no known grave. Of the crew of AJ-K, the body of Flt Sgt L. McDowell was the only one to be recovered from the sea.* (Author)

Sgt Guy Pegler RAF, 21 (Bath, Som.)

Sgt Thomas Jaye RAFVR, 21 (Crook, Co. Durham)

Plt Off Leonard George Weller RAFVR, 28 (Harpenden, Herts)

WO2 James Lamb Arthur RCAF, 25 (Coldwater, Ontario)

Sgt William Charles Arthur Long RAFVR, 19 (Bournemouth, Hants)

WO2 Joseph Gordon Brady RCAF, 27 (Ponoka, Alberta)

THE PRISONERS OF WAR

Plt Off Jim Fraser RCAF (AJ-M) – Stalag Luft 3, Sagan and Belaria

Plt Off Anthony Burcher DFM, RAAF (AJ-M) – Stalag Luft 3, Sagan and Belaria

Sgt Fred Tees (AJ-C) – Stalag Luft 6, Heydekrug

THE ABORTED SORTIES

Flt Lt Les Munro

AJ-W, ED921/G hit by light flak on the outward flight crossing Vlieland, Holland, damaging the VHF radio and intercom. Landed back at Scampton 00.30hrs with mine still onboard.

Flg Off Geoff Rice

AJ-H, ED936/G hit the sea on the outward flight near Vlieland, ripping off the Upkeep mine and tearing a hole in the bomb bay. Landed back at Scampton 00.50hrs.

Flt Sgt Cyril Anderson

AJ-Y, ED924/G experienced navigational difficulties and malfunction of rear turret. Turned back over Germany at 03.10hrs without dropping mine. Landed back at Scampton 05.30hrs with mine still on board.

What Happened to the Dams Raid Survivors?

Of the 133 men who set out on the dams raid, 77 returned; and of these survivors, 32 were destined not to see out the war's end. They include Wg Cdr Guy Gibson and his entire crew. Most of these men were still serving with 617 Squadron at the time of their deaths, but in the cases of Gibson, Flt Sgt Anderson, Flt Lt Trevor-Roper and Flg Off Jagger, they had moved to other squadrons in Bomber Command. Their names are listed below.

617 Sqn, KIA, Ladbergen (Dortmund-Ems Canal), 14–15 September 1943
Sqn Ldr D.J.H. Maltby, Sgt W. Hatton, Flt Sgt V. Nicholson, Flg Off J. Fort, Flt Sgt A.J. Stone, Flt Sgt V. Hill, Sgt H.T. Simmonds.

617 Sqn, KIA, Ladbergen (Dortmund-Ems Canal), 15–16 September 1943
Flt Lt L.G. Knight, Flt Lt T.H. Taerum, Flg Off F.M. Spafford, Flt Lt R.E.G. Hutchison, Plt Off G.A. Deering, Sgt D. Allatson, Sgt D.J.D. Powell.

49 Sqn, KIA, Mannheim, 23–24 September 1943
Flt Sgt C.T. Anderson, Sgts D. Paterson, L. Nugent, D. Bickle, G.J. Green, A. Ewan and R. Black.

617 Sqn, KIA, Liège, 20–21 December 1943
Flt Sgt E.C. Smith, Flg Off R. MacFarlane, WO2 J.W. Thrasher, WO2 C.B. Gowrie, Flt Sgt T.W. Maynard, Flt Sgt S. Burns.

617 Sqn, KIA, Antheor Viaduct, 12–13 February 1944
Flt Lt R.C. Hay.

617 Sqn, killed in flying accident, 13 February 1944
Sgt J. Pulford.

97 Sqn, KIA Nuremberg, 30–31 March 1944
Flt Lt R.A.D. Trevor-Roper.

460 Sqn, killed in training accident, 30 April 1944
Flg Off B. Jagger.

627 Sqn, KIA, Rheydt, 19–20 September 1944
Wg Cdr G.P. Gibson.
KIA = Killed in Action

OPPOSITE *Sqn Ldr David Maltby (one of Gibson's flight commanders on the dams raid) and his dams raid crew, and Flt Lt Les Knight and four of Gibson's dams raid crew (Taerum, Spafford, Hutchison and Deering), with Sgt Dennis Powell (of Bill Townsend's crew) and Daniel Allatson (of Ken Brown's crew), were killed in two consecutive raids on the Dortmund-Ems Canal on 14-15 and 15-16 September 1943. The canal had been the focus of many Bomber Command attacks until it was successfully breached by Lancasters of 617 Squadron using 12,000lb Tallboy deep penetration bombs on 23-24 September 1944. Breaches were made in the banks of two parallel branches of the canal, causing a six-mile stretch to be drained.* (IWM C4667)

What Happened to the Aircraft That Survived the Dams Raid?

ED825 (AJ-T)	Missing, arms supply drop to SOE target in northern France, 10-12-43. Hit by flak when flying at low level and crashed.
ED886 (AJ-O)	Missing, arms supply drop to SOE target in northern France, 10-12-43. Hit by flak and crashed at Terramesnil, Somme.
ED906 (AJ-J)	To 61 Sqn, 08-46. SOC 29-07-47.
ED909 (AJ-P)	To 61 Sqn. Instructional airframe 6242M. SOC 29-07-47.
ED912 (AJ-N)	To 46 MU, 02-45. SOC 29-06-46.
ED918 (AJ-F)	Struck sea and crashed into sea wall, Snettisham, Norfolk, on practice low-level night bombing exercise, 20-01-44.
ED921 (AJ-W)	Damaged 17-08-44. Stored 46 MU. SOC 26-09-47.
ED924 (AJ-Y)	Damaged 02-07-44. Stored 46 MU. SOC 23-09-46.
ED929 (AJ-L)	Stored 46 MU, 01-45. SOC 07-10-46.
ED932 (AJ-G)	To 61 Sqn. SOC 29-07-47.
ED936 (AJ-H)	Damaged 21-07-44. SOC 28-07-44.

KEY
MU = Maintenance Unit
SOC = Struck off Charge (scrapped)
SOE = Special Operations Executive

BIBLIOGRAPHY

Documents

The National Archives, Kew
AIR 2/4890 Award Citation for A/Wg Cdr Guy Gibson
AIR 2/4967 Award Citation for Flt Sgt Ken Brown

Books

Air Publication 2062A, *Pilot's and Flight Engineer's Notes: Lancaster I, III and X* (Air Ministry, 1944)

Babington-Smith, Constance, *Evidence in Camera* (London, Chatto and Windus, 1958)

Brickhill, Paul, *The Dam Busters* (London, Evans, 1951)

Chorley, W.R., *RAF Bomber Command Losses of the Second World War 1943* (Leicester, Midland Counties Publications, 1996)

Dictionary of National Biography, 1951–60, 1971–80

Euler, Helmuth, *The Dams Raid through the Lens* (London, Battle of Britain International, 2001)

Falconer, Jonathan, *Bomber Command in Fact, Film and Fiction* (Stroud, Sutton, 1996)

Gibson, Guy, *Enemy Coast Ahead* (London, Michael Joseph, 1946)

Hastings, Max, *Bomber Command* (London, Michael Joseph, 1979)

Leaf, Edward, *Above All Unseen: The RAF's Photographic Reconnaissance Units 1939–1945* (Sparkford, PSL, 1997)

Lumsden, Alec, *Wellington Special* (Shepperton, Ian Allan, 1974)

MacBean, John A., and Hogben, Arthur S., *Bombs Gone: The development and use of British air-dropped weapons from 1912 to the present day* (Wellingborough, PSL, 1990)

Mason, Francis K., *The Avro Lancaster* (Bourne End, Aston Publications, 1989)

Morris, Richard, *Guy Gibson* (London, Viking, 1994)

Nesbit, Roy Conyers, *Eyes of the RAF: A History of Photo-Reconnaissance* (Stroud, Sutton, 1996)

Speer, Albert, *Inside the Third Reich* (London, Weidenfeld & Nicolson, 1970)

Sweetman, John, *The Dambusters Raid*, 2nd Edition (London, Jane's, 1990)

Tubbs, D.B., *Lancaster Bomber* (London, Pan/Ballantine, 1972)

Journal and Magazine Articles

'The Dam Busting Weapon', Dr B.N. Wallis, *Air Clues*, May 1963

'The Origins and Design of the Attack on the German Dams', A.R. Collins, *Proceedings of the Institution of Civil Engineers*, Pt 2, June 1982, Vol. 73

'Photography of the Dams', *Coastal Command Quarterly Review* (n.d., c.1943)

'The Dams Raid and After', Alfred Price, *Purnell's History of the Second World War*, Vol. II, No. 10

'The Ruhr Dams Raid 1943', *After the Battle*, No. 3, 1973

'Dam Busters: The Film', François Prins, *FlyPast*, October 1985

'The Last Dambuster', Jack Meadows, *Aeroplane Monthly*, May 2000

Newspaper Obituaries

The Times, 17 March 1954, Joseph 'Mutt' Summers
Daily Telegraph, 31 October 1979, Sir Barnes Wallis
The Times, 4 November 1988, Sir Mick Martin
Daily Telegraph, 22 October 1990, Sir Ben Lockspeiser
The Times, 28 September 1998, Joe McCarthy

Websites

www.cwgc.org – The Commonwealth War Graves Commission, Debt of Honour Register
www.bundesarchiv.de – Bundesarchiv
www.iwm.org.uk – Imperial War Museum
www.rafmuseum.org.uk – RAF Museum

INDEX